Spelling and Vocabulary Skills

Level 4

A Division of The McGraw-Hill Companies

Columbus, Ohio

www.sra4kids.com

SRA/McGraw-Hill

A Division of The **McGraw·Hill** *Companies*

Send all inquiries to:
SRA/McGraw Hill
4400 Easton Commons
Columbus, OH 43219

Printed in the United States of America.

ISBN 0-07-571105-2

20 21 22 23 HSO 14 13 12 11

Table of Contents

Unit 6 A Changing America

Name _____ Date _____

Context Clues

Context clues are clues in a sentence or paragraph that help you find the meaning of a word. How the word is used in a sentence will give you a clue to the meaning.

 **Try It!** Use the following words to complete each sentence with the correct word from the story.

abreast	capacity	literally	dubiously	prospect

1. When at length she came _____ of the barn, she saw the cattle wire fence that marked the other end of the pasture.

2. The size of the brain is no measure of its _____.

3. When the crow told Mrs. Frisby that he would drop her off, Mrs. Frisby thought he _____ meant he would drop her while flying in the air.

4. "Come down here," she said. "I'll get the string off." "How?" said the crow _____.

5. She could go home by the same roundabout way she had come, in which case she would surely end up walking alone in the woods in the dark—a frightening _____, for at night the forest was alive with danger.

▶ **Context Clues**

Practice

Find the meaning of the words.

6. abreast _____

7. capacity _____

8. literally _____

9. dubiously _____

10. prospect _____

How did you find the meaning of each word?

11. _____

12. _____

13. _____

14. _____

15. _____

After finding the meanings of the words, use them in sentences.

16. abreast _____

17. capacity _____

18. literally _____

19. dubiously _____

20. prospect _____

VOCABULARY

Short-Vowel Sounds

Word List

1. victims
2. pasture
3. bottomless
4. shrubs
5. silver
6. cactus
7. lettuce
8. doctor
9. principle
10. cockpit
11. minimum
12. billion
13. hundred
14. contact
15. rustic

Selection Words

16. windmill
17. traffic
18. tablet
19. solid
20. punish

Pattern Study

The short-vowel sound is usually **between two consonants** in syllables.

Break the following words into syllables. Concentrating on the first syllable of the word, identify it as a **CVC** or **CCVC** pattern. Some words may have only one syllable. The first one is done for you.

1. vic•tims CVC
2. _____
3. _____
4. _____
5. _____
6. _____
7. _____
8. _____
9. _____
10. _____

11. _____
12. _____
13. _____
14. _____
15. _____
16. _____
17. _____
18. _____
19. _____
20. _____

UNIT I Risks and Consequences • **Lesson I** *Mrs. Frisby and the Crow*

▶ **Short-Vowel Sounds**

Strategies

 Proofreading Strategy **While reading through the sentences, look for the different types of spelling errors. Underline the misspelled words and spell the words correctly on the lines provided.**

21. Rush hour is usually when trafic is the heaviest. _____

22. A cacktus is a plant that can be found in North and South America and some parts of Africa. _____

23. Medicine often comes in the form of tablits or capsules.

_____

24. After moving to another city, it is nice of you to stay in contack with old friends. _____

25. Sillver is an expensive metal. _____

26. Crime victems should report the crime that was committed against them to the police. _____

27. A docter must study for a long time before he or she can practice medicine. _____

28. A prinspel of the American government is equal treatment for all people. _____

29. Some of the richest people in the world are worth more than a bilion dollars. _____

30. A minemum of ten pennies is required in exchange for a dime.

_____

SPELLING

External Context Clues

External context clues are words in a sentence that tell you the meaning of another word in the same sentence.

 **Read the following sentences. Beneath the sentence, write the meaning of the word that is underlined in the sentence.**

Example: After my dog has her babies, I will give one of the puppies to Mrs. Quinn.

Puppies are baby dogs.

1. We used a rope to <u>moor</u> the sailboat to the dock.

_____

2. The cowhand told us that the <u>lasso</u> wasn't long enough to reach the animals. The loop on the rope was also too small, he said.

_____

3. The <u>journalist's</u> assignment from the newspaper was to write a story about my grandmother for tomorrow's newspaper.

_____

4. The thunder made the house <u>quake</u>. As a result of the house trembling, there are cracks in the walls.

_____

5. The butcher asked me to repair his <u>cleaver</u>. The short handle was broken and the broad blade needed to be sharpened. The butcher told me he needed his cleaver to cut meat.

_____

UNIT I Risks and Consequences • **Lesson 2** *Toto*

▶ **Semantic Context Clues**

⟦ Practice ⟧

Semantic clues are clues authors use to help you find the meaning of a word. A semantic clue can be a definition, or it can be an appositive. Sometimes it is signaled by words such as *or*, *that is to say*, and *in other words*.

Circle the words that help you understand what the underlined words mean.

Example: Over time the wood had petrified, or (turned to stone).

6. Omri learned that one of his ancestors had been Louis the Fourteenth of France. In other words, Omri could trace the people on his family tree back over many generations to the Sun King!

7. Unfortunately for Mr. Wilkins, his new glasses gave his face a haughty look, as though he felt superior to all those around him.

8. Warren watched enviously as Maryanne rode her new bike, jealous that he was still too young for a two-wheeler.

9. The game warden was on the trail of a poacher, a person who illegally kills wild animals.

10. Have you ever seen a truly menacing storm? By that I mean a storm so frightening that you fear for the safety of the ship.

Use each word in a sentence.

11. ancestors _____

12. haughty _____

13. enviously _____

14. poacher _____

15. menacing _____

VOCABULARY

The /ā/ Sound

Word List

1. neighbor
2. weigh
3. eighth
4. crayon
5. sway
6. stray
7. erase
8. female
9. grain
10. trail
11. male
12. state
13. bacon
14. basement
15. chamber

Selection Words

16. midday
17. brave
18. claim
19. sailed
20. plains

Pattern Study

The *_ay* spelling for /ā/ is found at the end of a word or syllable, and the *ai_* spelling is found in the middle of a word.

▸ Write the words with the /ā/ sound spelled *a*.

1. _____   2. _____

▸ Write the words with the /ā/ sound spelled *a_e*.

3. _____   6. _____

4. _____   7. _____

5. _____   8. _____

▸ Write the words with the /ā/ sound spelled *ai_*.

9. _____   12. _____

10. _____   13. _____

11. _____

▸ Write the words with the /ā/ sound spelled *_ay*.

14. _____   16. _____

15. _____   17. _____

▸ Write the words with the /ā/ sound spelled *eigh*.

18. _____   20. _____

19. _____

▶ **The /ā/ Sound**

Strategies

Visualization Strategy   Write five words that end in *ay*. The first one is done for you.

21. ____*say*____   24. _____

22. _____   25. _____

23. _____

Write five words that end in *ail*. The first one is done for you.

26. ____*snail*____   29. _____

27. _____   30. _____

28. _____

Write five words that end in *ain*. The first one is done for you.

31. ____*train*____   34. _____

32. _____   35. _____

33. _____

SPELLING

UNIT 1   Risks and Consequences • **Lesson 3** *Sarah Plain and Tall*

Word Structure

There are different parts of a word: prefixes, suffixes, and roots.

▶ Prefix—an addition to the beginning of the word (*re*call)

▶ Suffix—an addition to the end of the word (call*ing*)

▶ Root word—a word to which a prefix and a suffix can be added (re*call*ed)

Use the vocabulary words to practice word structure.

▶ **curl**—to form into a curved (ring) shape

▶ **shingle**—building material used to cover the roof or the sides of a building

▶ **impress**—to have a strong effect on the mind or feelings

▶ **shuffle**—to move around

Try It!   Identify the underlined section of each word as a prefix, suffix, or root word.

1. curl<u>ing</u>   _____

2. un<u>curl</u>ed   _____

3. shingl<u>ed</u>   _____

4. re<u>shing</u>led   _____

5. <u>re</u>shingle   _____

6. impress<u>ive</u>   _____

7. re<u>shuffl</u>ed   _____

▶ **Word Structure**

Practice

Use the correct word in each sentence.

curling	curled	shingled	reshingled
impressive	shuffle	reshuffled	uncurl

8. After the shingles fell off the roof, my dad _____ the roof by putting them back on.

9. I want the person who curled the rope around the tree to

please _____ it.

10. If we don't _____ the cards, they will be in the same order they were yesterday.

11. The new building downtown is quite _____.

12. She _____ her hair because she did not like it straight.

Compound words are words made of two or more smaller words. Separate each compound word into two words.

Example: anyone *any*   *one*

13. hearthstones _____ _____

14. homemade _____ _____

15. shuffleboard _____ _____

VOCABULARY

The /ē/ Sound

Word List

1. steel
2. fleet
3. seaweed
4. wreath
5. measles
6. scream
7. least
8. yield
9. shield
10. shriek
11. thief
12. donkey
13. hockey
14. trolley
15. niece

Selection Words

16. prairie
17. eager
18. seals
19. married
20. sneak

Pattern Study

/ē/ is often spelled *e*, *e_e*, *ee*, *ea*, *_ie_*, and *_y*.

▶ Write the words with the /ē/ sound spelled *ee*.

1. _____   3. _____

2. _____

▶ Write the words with the /ē/ sound spelled *ea*.

4. _____   8. _____

5. _____   9. _____

6. _____   10. _____

7. _____   11. _____

▶ Write the words with the /ē/ sound spelled *_ie_*.

12. _____   16. _____

13. _____   17. _____

14. _____   18. _____

15. _____

▶ Write the words with the /ē/ sound spelled *ey*.

19. _____   21. _____

20. _____

UNIT I Risks and Consequences • **Lesson 3** *Sarah Plain and Tall*

► **The /ē/ Sound**

Strategies

Vizualization Strategy Complete each set of words with one or two words from the /ē/ spelling list.

22. yell   scream   _____ , _____

23. stop   wait   _____ _____

24. ocean   grass   _____ _____

25. mule   horse   _____ _____

26. sports   ice skates   _____ _____

Fill in the /ē/ spelling pattern that is missing in each word. Then rewrite the word.

27. th_____f   _____

28. _____ger   _____

29. s_____ls   _____

30. marr_____d   _____

THE DAILY COMET

SPELLING

UNIT 1 Risks and Consequences • **Lesson 4** *Escape*

Dictionary

Entry words appear in alphabetical order in the dictionary. If two words begin with the same letter, the second letter determines the alphabetical order. Sometimes, both the first and second letters in two words are the same. Then the third letter determines the order of the words, and so on.

The dictionary will indicate what part of speech a word is— noun (n.), verb (v.), adverb (adv.), adjective (adj.) and so on.

Try It! Write the part of speech for each word. The first one is done for you.

1. perspiration *noun*
2. trough _____
3. asparagus _____
4. scythes _____
5. reconsider _____

Write the words you find in your dictionary directly before and after each of these words.

6. _____ perspiration _____

7. _____ trough _____

8. _____ asparagus _____

9. _____ scythes _____

10. _____ reconsider _____

Practice

Many words have more than one meaning. Find the meaning of the following words in the dictionary, then write two sentences for each word. For the first sentence, use the first meaning listed in your dictionary. For the second sentence, use the second meaning listed in your dictionary. If there is only one meaning for a word, write two sentences using the only meaning listed.

11. perspiration _____

_____

_____

12. trough _____

_____

_____

13. asparagus _____

_____

_____

14. scythes _____

_____

_____

15. reconsider _____

_____

_____

VOCABULARY

UNIT 1 **Risks and Consequences • Lesson 4** *Escape*

The /ō/ Sound

Word List

1. over
2. blow
3. coast
4. cobra
5. elbow
6. bulldozer
7. overflow
8. narrow
9. window
10. shadow
11. hollow
12. groan
13. stow
14. bowl
15. coax

Selection Words

16. whole
17. know
18. swallow
19. grindstones
20. commotion

Pattern Study

/ō/ is spelled *o*, *o_e*, *oa_*, and *_ow* as in *pony*, *bone*, *boat*, and *snow*.

▶ Write the words with the /ō/ sound spelled *o*.

1. _____ 3. _____

2. _____ 4. _____

▶ Write the words with the /ō/ sound spelled *o_e*.

5. _____ 7. _____

6. _____

▶ Write the words with the /ō/ sound spelled *oa_*.

8. _____ 10. _____

9. _____

▶ Write the words with the /ō/ sound spelled *_ow*.

11. _____ 17. _____

12. _____ 18. _____

13. _____ 19. _____

14. _____ 20. _____

15. _____ 21. _____

16. _____

▶ **The /ō/ Sound**

Practice

 Pronunciation Strategy Divide each of the spelling words into syllables.

over *o•ver*

22. cobra _____ 28. shadow _____

23. elbow _____ 29. hollow _____

24. bulldozer _____ 30. over _____

25. overflow _____ 31. grindstone _____

26. narrow _____ 32. swallow _____

27. window _____ 33. commotion _____

 Pronunciation Strategy Divide the words according to the /ō/ or /o/ sounds.

	/ō/	/o/
34. slow	_____	_____
35. mow	_____	_____
36. got	_____	_____
37. goat	_____	_____
38. crow	_____	_____
39. mom	_____	_____
40. drop	_____	_____

SPELLING

UNIT 1 **Risks and Consequences • Lesson 5** *Mae Jemison: Space Scientist*

Thesaurus

A **thesaurus** is used to find synonyms, other words with similar meanings.

Use the vocabulary words to practice using a thesaurus.

▶ astronaut: a person who travels beyond Earth

▶ orbit: the path used by one celestial body as it moves around another

▶ gravity: the force that causes things to have weight

▶ satellite: a man-made object that moves around Earth and collects and stores information

▶ laboratories: places used for experimental study in science

 **Write the vocabulary word that fits with each group of words.**

1. space traveler, space pilot, rocket pilot, explorer

_____

2. space station, man-made moon, spy in the sky

_____

3. circle, round cycle, curve _____

4. workrooms, experiment rooms, testing rooms

_____

5. heaviness, pressure, force _____

Practice

Read each sentence to learn the meaning of the underlined word. Use a thesaurus to locate synonyms for each meaning. If you do not understand the meaning of the underlined word, you may use a dictionary. The first one is done for you.

6. The judge's decision was fair and <u>just</u>.

fair-minded, impartial

7. I have <u>just</u> the right amount of sugar for my tea.

_____

8. I <u>rank</u> fourth in my class in height.

_____

9. The cheese became <u>rank</u> after a month.

_____

10. I wrote a <u>note</u> to my father.

_____

11. We should <u>note</u> that words may have more than one meaning.

_____

VOCABULARY

The /ī/ Sound

Word List

1. dynamite
2. flight
3. knight
4. pirate
5. tighten
6. type
7. style
8. rhyme
9. spite
10. supply
11. pilot
12. mile
13. midnight
14. icicle
15. skylight

Selection Words

16. decide
17. science
18. overnight
19. might
20. wired

Pattern Study

/ī/ is spelled *i*, *i_e*, *igh*, and *_y* as in *icy*, *site*, *high*, and *dry*.

▶ Write the words with the /ī/ sound spelled *i*.

1. _____   3. _____

2. _____   4. _____

▶ Write the words with the /ī/ sound spelled *i_e*.

5. _____   8. _____

6. _____   9. _____

7. _____

▶ Write the words with the /ī/ sound spelled *igh*.

10. _____   14. _____

11. _____   15. _____

12. _____   16. _____

13. _____

▶ Write the words with the /ī/ sound spelled *_y*.

17. _____   20. _____

18. _____   21. _____

19. _____   22. _____

▶ **The /ī/ Sound**

Strategies

Visualization Strategy

Write five words that end in *ight*.

23. _____   26. _____

24. _____   27. _____

25. _____

Write two words that end in *ired*.

28. _____   29. _____

Write three words that end in *ile*.

30. _____   32. _____

31. _____

Write three words that end in *ite*.

33. _____   35. _____

34. _____

SPELLING

UNIT I Risks and Consequences • **Lesson 6** *Two Tickets to Freedom*

Review: External Context Clues

Context clues are found in a paragraph or sentence and help you define an unknown word.

▶ **abolitionist**—a person who was in favor of ending slavery

▶ **console**—to comfort or cheer a person

▶ **liberty**—to act, think, or speak the way you please

▶ **agitated**—feeling disturbed

▶ **predicament**—a difficult situation

Try It! **Complete each sentence with one of the vocabulary words listed above.**

1. During bad times, William _____ himself with the thought that God, who had been so good as to allow them to come this far, would not let them be turned aside now.

2. The conductor, who may well have been an _____, thought he could tease the Southern slaveowner.

3. Ellen was in a _____ for another reason. She had no money at all.

4. The conductor, believing that William was a slave, asked

   William if he wanted his _____ after a month.

5. William became _____ when he thought the conductor would throw him off the train.

UNIT 1   Risks and Consequences • **Lesson 6** *Two Tickets to Freedom*

Practice

> **Prefix:** A group of meaningful letters that can be added to the beginning of a word (equal, un-equal)
>
> **Suffix:** A group of meaningful letters that can be added to the end of a word (play, play-ing)
>
> **Roots:** A word to which prefixes or suffixes are added (curl, un-curl-ed)
>
> **Compound Words:** A word made of two or more smaller words (hearth-stones)

Write the words in parts then circle the prefix in each word.

6. rewrite _____

7. disagree _____

8. deform _____

Write the words in parts then circle the suffix in each word.

9. ducking _____

10. walked _____

Write the words in parts then circle the root word.

11. reinvented _____

12. unanswered _____

Break the compound words into two smaller words.

13. toenail _____

14. softball _____

UNIT I Risks and Consequences • **Lesson 6** *Two Tickets to Freedom*

The /o͞o/ and /ū/ Sounds

Word List

1. value
2. lose
3. cue
4. bruise
5. proof
6. smooth
7. suit
8. truce
9. boost
10. true
11. reuse
12. crew
13. fruit
14. juice
15. issue

Selection Words

16. flute
17. whose
18. view
19. continued
20. include

Pattern Study

The _ue and _ew spellings of the /o͞o/ and /ū/ sounds do not occur at the beginning of a word.

▶ Write the words with the /o͞o/ sound spelled u_e.

1. _____ 3. _____

2. _____

▶ Write the words with the /o͞o/ and /ū/ sounds spelled _ue and _ew.

4. _____ 7. _____

5. _____ 8. _____

6. _____ 9. _____

▶ Write the words with the /o͞o/ sound spelled oo.

10. _____ 12. _____

11. _____

▶ Write the words with the /o͞o/ sound spelled ui.

13. _____ 15. _____

14. _____ 16. _____

UNIT I **Risks and Consequences • Lesson 6** *Two Tickets to Freedom*

▶ The /o͞o/ and /u̅/ Sounds

Strategies

 Proofreading Strategy Circle the misspelled words in the sentences. Write the correct spelling on the line provided.

17. I have a broose on my left leg. _____

18. Some music is written especially for the flut. _____

19. I love fresh orange juce. _____

20. The ring of the telephone was the actor's cu to go on stage. _____

21. An orange is a citrus frut. _____

22. My seafood salad did not inclood vegetables. _____

23. We tried to help our neighbor whos dog had run away. _____

24. He places great valu on her friendship. _____

25. The people who work on and run a ship are called the crue. _____

26. The teacher's praise gave me a bost. _____

27. The sailors got their first vew of land after many weeks at sea.

_____

SPELLING

UNIT I Risks and Consequences • **Lesson 7** *Daedalus and Icarus*

Review: Dictionary and Thesaurus

A **dictionary** gives definitions, or meanings of words, and shows their related forms, parts of speech, and word history.

A **thesaurus** uses synonyms and sometimes antonyms to define words.

 **Try It!** Use a dictionary to find the part of speech for each word. Write the part of speech for each word. The first one is done for you.

1. delectable   *adj.*_____

2. luxurious   _____

3. daub   _____

4. hurtle   _____

5. vault   _____

rotten	feeble	anger	help	annoy

Complete each pair with a synonym from the box.

6. assist   _____

7. decayed   _____

8. vex   _____

9. fury   _____

10. flimsy   _____

UNIT I Risks and Consequences • **Lesson 7** *Daedalus and Icarus*

Dictionary and Thesaurus

Practice

Write the vocabulary word that fits with each group of words.

luxurious	delectable	vault	daub	hurtle

11. delicious, tasty, yummy _____

12. rich, splendid _____

13. rush, race, speed _____

14. smeared, plastered, dabbed _____

15. roof, ceiling _____

Use a thesaurus to find other words that represent the following words.

16. spout _____

17. freeze _____

18. swell _____

19. nibble _____

20. blunder _____

VOCABULARY

Name _____ Date _____

Review: Vowel Sounds

Word List

1. chamber
2. steel
3. swallow
4. brain
5. neighbor
6. erase
7. seaweed
8. donkey
9. shriek
10. cobra
11. bulldozer
12. shadow
13. dynamite
14. style
15. spite

Selection Words

16. maze
17. floating
18. freedom
19. creature
20. least

Pattern Study

Long-vowel sounds /ā/, /ē/, /ī/, and /ō/ are spelled many ways.

▶Write the words with the /ā/ sound spelled *a, ai_, _ay,* or *a_e.*

1. _____   3. _____
2. _____   4. _____

▶Write the words with the /ē/ sound spelled *ee, ea,* or *_ie_.*

5. _____   8. _____
6. _____   9. _____
7. _____   10. _____

▶Write the words with the /ī/ sound spelled *_y.*

11. _____   12. _____

▶Write the words with the /ō/ sound spelled *o, o_e, oa_,* or *_ow.*

13. _____   16. _____
14. _____   17. _____
15. _____   18. _____

UNIT 1   Risks and Consequences • **Lesson 7** *Daedalus and Icarus*

▶ **Long-Vowel Sounds**

Practice

 Visualization Strategy Each word below has a long-vowel sound in it. Find the long-vowel sound and brainstorm for another word that has that same vowel sound. The first one is done for you.

19. steel   _____*feel*_____   **23.** jeered   _____

20. donkey   _____   **24.** floating   _____

21. spite   _____   **25.** least   _____

22. maze   _____

Write the spelling words formed by adding, dropping, or changing one or more vowels in each word. Use the spelling list on page 28 as a reference.

26. chumber _____   **32.** cobrae _____

27. swallew _____   **33.** bulldezer _____

28. braen _____   **34.** shaduw _____

29. neabor _____   **35.** dynamate _____

30. eraes _____   **36.** craeture _____

31. seawed _____   **37.** stile _____

SPELLING

UNIT 2 Dollars and Sense • **Lesson I** *Starting a Business*

Suffixes *-ly* and *-ing*

Adding *-ly* to the ends of words creates adverbs, which describe the way something occurs. *(swiftly, expertly)*
If a word ends in *y*, the *y* is changed to *i* before adding *-ly*. *(lucky, luckily)*
The *-ing* ending shows that something is happening right now. *(dancing)*
For words ending in *e,* drop the *e* before adding *-ing*. *(practice, practicing)*
For words ending in a short vowel sound plus *p* or *t*, the final consonant is usually doubled before adding *-ing*. *(nap, napping; hit, hitting)*

 **Remove the suffixes *-ing* and *-ly* from the following words and write the words correctly on the lines provided.**

1. manufacturing _____

2. analyzing _____

3. partially _____

4. brainstorming _____

5. speedily _____

UNIT 2 Dollars and Sense • **Lesson I** *Starting a Business*

▶ Suffixes *-ly* and *-ing*

VOCABULARY

Practice

**Complete each sentence with the correct form of
each word.**

6. I am (**manufacture, manufacturing**)

   _____ the product.

7. For homework I have to (**analyze, analyzing**)

   _____ the reading passage on dogs
   and cats.

8. I created a (**realistic, realistically**)

   _____ painting of life on the
   school playground.

9. I am (**brainstorming, brainstorm**)

   _____ for words that rhyme with *straw*.

10. A person who is (**artistic, artistically**)

    _____ has a special gift.

Write the vocabulary word that fits with each sentence.

manufacturing	analyzing	realistic
artistic	brainstorming	

11. The process of making something: _____

12. Showing a creative talent or skill: _____

13. Thinking of many different ideas: _____

14. Appearing as in everyday life: _____

15. Studying something carefully: _____

UNIT 2 Dollars and Sense • **Lesson 1** *Starting a Business*

The /ə/ Sound

Word List

1. watermelon
2. season
3. reason
4. horizon
5. happen
6. opinion
7. custom
8. crimson
9. garden
10. mitten
11. person
12. kitten
13. dungeon
14. problem
15. button

Selection Words

16. lessons
17. preparation
18. vacation
19. obligations
20. customer

Pattern Study

The /ə/ sound is the vowel sound in the unstressed syllable of a word.

Rewrite each word on the lines provided and circle the letter(s) that spell the /ə/ sound in each word. Some words may contain more than one /ə/ sound. You may use a dictionary. The first one is done for you.

1. wa•ter•me•lon   wa•t(e)r•me•l(o)n

2. sea•son   _____

3. rea•son   _____

4. ho•ri•zon   _____

5. hap•pen   _____

6. o•pin•ion   _____

7. cus•tom   _____

8. crim•son   _____

9. gar•den   _____

10. mit•ten   _____

11. per•son   _____

12. kit•ten   _____

13. dun•geon   _____

14. prob•lem   _____

15. but•ton   _____

UNIT 2 **Dollars and Sense • Lesson I** *Starting a Business*

▶ **The /ə/ Sound**

Strategies

 Pronunciation Strategy Write the words on the lines provided and separate them into syllables using dots between each syllable. The first one is done for you.

16. lessons   les•sons _____

17. preparation _____

18. vacation _____

19. obligations _____

20. customer _____

When you say a long word, you say parts of it with more force than you do others. You say the first part of the word *breakfast* with more force than the second part. You say the second part of the word *tonight* with more force than the first. This kind of force is called *stress*. Most dictionaries use accent marks (´) to show which part to say with more force. An accent mark comes after the part that is spoken with the most stress.

Write the words on the lines provided and separate them into syllables using dots between each syllable. Circle the stressed syllable in each word.

21. lessons _____

22. preparation _____

23. vacation _____

24. obligations _____

25. customer _____

UNIT 2   **Dollars and Sense • Lesson 2** *Henry Wells and William G. Fargo*

Antonyms

> Antonyms are words that mean the opposite or almost the opposite of other words.
>
> **good** and **bad**
>
> **tall** and **short**

Try It!   **After reading the passage, write one antonym for each underlined word.**

About fifty percent of Americans are overweight. An overweight person can lose weight by doing <u>proper</u> exercises, like walking, and eating healthful foods, like fruits and vegetables. Every person, <u>young</u> and old, should exercise and eat healthful foods, even if they don't want to lose weight. Whether or not you want to lose weight, it's a good idea to keep exercising so your muscles stay <u>firm</u>. Remember, it's okay to want to be <u>slender</u>, but not every person is built to be the same size. Weight loss is not a <u>rapid</u> process, so do not expect to lose a lot of weight in a short period of time.

1. proper   _____

2. young   _____

3. firm   _____

4. slender   _____

5. rapid   _____

UNIT 2   Dollars and Sense • **Lesson 2** *Henry Wells and William G. Fargo*

▶ Antonyms

VOCABULARY

(**Practice**)

An analogy is two pairs of words that are related in the same way.

▶ **Front** is to **back** as **left** is to **right.**

Front is the opposite of back and left is the opposite of right. This is an antonym analogy.

▶ **Happy** is to **sad** as **hurry** is to **slow.**

▶ **Hot** is to **cold** as **full** is to **empty.**

Complete the antonym analogies with a word from inside the parentheses.

6. **Lost** is to **found** as **outside** is to _____.
   (indoors, inside, home)

7. **Keep** is to **give** as **enjoyment** is to _____.
   (displeasure, hate, unlike)

8. **Bad** is to **good** as **destroy** is to _____.
   (create, nice, form)

9. **Noisy** is to **quiet** as **appoint** is to _____.
   (dismiss, stop, pause)

10. **Positive** is to **negative** as **ground** is to _____.
    (sky, flower, rain)

Use these words to create antonym analogies.

11. rapid _____

12. firm _____

13. proper _____

14. young _____

15. slender _____

Name _____ Date _____

The /ow/ and /oi/ Sounds

Word List

1. account
2. trousers
3. rejoice
4. poison
5. outside
6. ground
7. enjoyment
8. destroy
9. employ
10. appoint
11. bounce
12. about
13. tower
14. plow
15. joint

Selection Words

16. founder
17. amount
18. bound
19. choice
20. mountain

Pattern Study

The /ow/ sound is spelled *ou_* and *ow*; the /oi/ sound is spelled *oi* and *_oy*.

▶ Write the words with the /ow/ sound spelled *ou_*.

1. _____   6. _____

2. _____   7. _____

3. _____   8. _____

4. _____   9. _____

5. _____   10. _____

▶ Write the words with the /ow/ sound spelled *ow*.

11. _____   12. _____

▶ Write the words with the /oi/ sound spelled *oi*.

13. _____   16. _____

14. _____   17. _____

15. _____

▶ Write the words with the /oi/ sound spelled *_oy*.

18. _____   20. _____

19. _____

UNIT 2 **Dollars and Sense • Lesson 2** *Henry Wells and William G. Fargo*

▶ **The /ow/ and /oi/ Sounds**

SPELLING

Strategies

 Visualization Strategy Circle the word that is spelled correctly.

21. choise   choice   choyce

22. poison   poyson   pouson

23. touer   toyer   tower

24. destroi   destroy   destorie

25. jouint   joyint   joint

 Visualization Strategy Complete each spelling word with the letters *oy*, *oi*, *ou*, or *ow*. Write the correct word on the lines provided.

26. destr _____   _____

27. empl _____   _____

28. app _____ nt   _____

29. b _____ nce   _____

30. ab _____ t   _____

31. t _____ er   _____

32. pl _____   _____

33. p _____ son   _____

34. tr _____ sers   _____

35. rej _____ ce   _____

Name _____ Date _____

UNIT 2 **Dollars and Sense • Lesson 3** *Elias Sifuentes, Restaurateur*

Shades of Meaning

Different words can have shades of meaning that relate to similar emotions or feelings. Most of the time these words are adjectives, such as **hungry, starving,** and **famished.**

▶ I am **hungry** because I skipped lunch.

▶ I am **starving** because I skipped lunch and dinner.

▶ I am **famished** because I had nothing to eat all day.

| moist | stare | jog | furious | sometimes |

 **Try It!** **Complete each group with a word from the box.**

1. walk   _____   run

2. _____   wet   soaked

3. irritated   angry   _____

4. glance   watch   _____

5. _____   rarely   never

▶ **Shades of Meaning**

Practice

gigantic	warm	solitary	pinch	rapid
giggle	cupful	nobody	few	spoonful

Complete each group with a word from the box.

6. smile   _____   laugh

7. large   great   _____

8. quick   _____   speedy

9. _____   hot   scorching

Complete each sentence with a word from the box.

10. _____ people live to be one hundred years old.

11. He was the _____ hiker on the trail.

12. I rang the bell but _____ answered.

13. I added a _____ of sugar to my tea.

14. My mom added a _____ of flour to the cake mix.

15. Sarah added a _____ of salt to her soup.

VOCABULARY

UNIT 2 Dollars and Sense • **Lesson 3** *Elias Sifuentes, Restaurateur*

The /er/ Sound

Word List

1. worth
2. burst
3. birth
4. urgent
5. urge
6. thirst
7. serve
8. search
9. purpose
10. perfect
11. learn
12. heard
13. further
14. earnest
15. early

Selection Words

16. operator
17. sailor
18. shower
19. pearl
20. partner

Pattern Study

The /er/ sound can be spelled five different ways: *er, ear, ir, or,* and *ur.*

▶ Write the words with the /er/ sound spelled *er.*

1. _____ 4. _____
2. _____ 5. _____
3. _____ 6. _____

▶ Write the words with the /er/ sound spelled *ear.*

7. _____ 10. _____
8. _____ 11. _____
9. _____ 12. _____

▶ Write the words with the /er/ sound spelled *ir.*

13. _____ 14. _____

▶ Write the words with the /er/ sound spelled *or.*

15. _____ 17. _____
16. _____

▶ Write the words with the /er/ sound spelled *ur.*

18. _____ 21. _____
19. _____ 22. _____
20. _____

UNIT 2 **Dollars and Sense • Lesson 3** *Elias Sifuentes, Restaurateur*

The /er/ Sound

Strategies

 Visualization Strategy Use the letters in the following words to create a three or four-letter word.

23. operator _____

24. circle _____

25. shower _____

26. pearl _____

27. partner _____

 Visualization Strategy Write the spelling words formed by adding, dropping, or changing the highlighted letters in the following words.

28. purp**u**se _____

29. o**p**irator _____

30. **h**earl _____

31. sh**a**wer _____

32. sur**v**e _____

33. p**i**rfect _____

34. **d**urst _____

35. w**a**rth _____

36. f**a**rther _____

SPELLING

UNIT 2 Dollars and Sense • **Lesson 4** *Food from the 'Hood: A Garden of Hope*

Synonyms

Synonyms are words that have similar meanings. **Read the following definitions and use these words to complete the exercise below.**
mural: a picture painted on a wall or ceiling
restoring: putting or bringing back together
riot: a disturbance of the public peace by three or more persons
confident: having trust or faith
occupation: the work a person does in order to earn a living.

 **Complete each set of synonyms with one vocabulary word.**

1. repairing, mending, fixing, _____

2. job, business, employment, _____

3. painting, photograph, scene, _____

4. confusion, commotion, disorder, _____

5. positive, certain, assured, _____

UNIT 2 Dollars and Sense • **Lesson 4** *Food from the 'Hood: A Garden of Hope*

▶ **Synonyms**

Practice

> An **analogy** is the relationship between two pairs of words.
>
> ▶ **Call** is to **shout** as **high** is to **tall.**
>
> This is a **synonym analogy.** The words **call** and **shout** are related to each other because they mean almost the same thing. The words **high** and **tall** are related to each other because they also mean almost the same thing.

Complete the following analogies with one of the words in the parentheses.

6. **Close** is to **shut** as **glare** is to _____.
   (answer, flash, talk)

7. **Divide** is to **separate** as **daring** is to _____.
   (timid, cold, bold)

8. **Go** is to **leave** as **clarify** is to _____.
   (talk, explain, read)

9. **City** is to **town** as **despair** is to _____.
   (happy, gloom, nice)

10. **Great** is to **large** as **narrate** is to _____.
    (describe, walk, run)

11. **Keep** is to **hold** as **nightmare** is to _____.
    (bad dream, sleep, wake)

12. **Right** is to **correct** as **prepare** is to _____.
    (arrange, account, move)

13. **Pain** is to **hurt** as **scare** is to _____.
    (unafraid, terror, happy)

14. **Late** is to **tardy** as **earned** is to _____.
    (deserved, took, fair)

VOCABULARY

UNIT 2 Dollars and Sense • **Lesson 4** *Food from the 'Hood: A Garden of Hope*

The /âr/ and /ar/ Sounds

Word List

1. glare
2. beware
3. daring
4. clarify
5. comparison
6. declare
7. despair
8. library
9. narrate
10. nightmare
11. prepare
12. repair
13. scare
14. spare
15. swear

Selection Words

16. carry
17. market
18. harvest
19. carpeting
20. scarf

Pattern Study

The **/âr/ sound** can be spelled *are* as in *care*, *ar* as in *dictionary*, *air* as in *fair*, or *ear* as in *wear*. The **/ar/ sound** is usually spelled *ar*, as in *far*.

▶ Write the words with the /âr/ sound spelled *are*.

1. _____ 5. _____

2. _____ 6. _____

3. _____ 7. _____

4. _____

▶ Write the words with the /âr/ sound spelled *air*.

8. _____ 9. _____

▶ Write the words with the /âr/ sound spelled *ar*.

10. _____ 13. _____

11. _____ 14. _____

12. _____ 15. _____

▶ Write the words with the /âr/ sound spelled *ear*.

16. _____

▶ Write the words with the /ar/ sound spelled *ar*.

17. _____ 19. _____

18. _____ 20. _____

UNIT 2 Dollars and Sense • **Lesson 4** *Food from the 'Hood: A Garden of Hope*

▶ /âr/ and /ar/ Sounds

Strategies

 Visualization Strategy Circle the word that is spelled correctly.

21. scair   scare   scere

22. carpeting   carepeting   carrpeting

23. harevest   harvist   harvest

24. scarf   scerf   skarf

25. dispair   despair   despere

 Vowel-Substitution Strategy Correct the spelling by changing the underlined vowel to the correct vowel. Write the correct word.

26. gl<u>e</u>re   _____

27. bew<u>e</u>re   _____

28. d<u>e</u>ring   _____

29. clar<u>e</u>fy   _____

30. comp<u>o</u>rison   _____

31. sp<u>e</u>re   _____

32. d<u>a</u>clare   _____

33. libr<u>e</u>ry   _____

34. n<u>e</u>rrate   _____

35. n<u>a</u>ghtm<u>e</u>re _____

SPELLING

Base Word Families

A base word is a word that can stand alone.

move

Base word families are the different forms you can make with a base word.

moveable, mover, moving, moved

Use the vocabulary words to learn how to use base word families.

- ▶ **research:** a study to find and learn things
- ▶ **tempt:** to give someone thoughts of doing something wrong or foolish
- ▶ **impair:** to lessen the quality or strength
- ▶ **invest:** to use money to buy something that will make more money
- ▶ **congratulate:** to wish a person well

 **Try It!**

Write the base word for each group of words.

1. researcher, researchable, researching, researched, _____

2. tempting, tempter, temptation, tempted, _____

3. impairment, impairing, impaired, _____

4. investment, investor, investable, _____

5. congratulations, congratulating, congratulated, _____

▶**Base Word Families**

{ **Practice** }

Complete each sentence with a word from inside the parentheses.

6. A history _____ may know a lot about the Constitution. (research, researcher)

7. We did _____ on the Internet before writing our report. (research, researcher)

8. Chocolate ice cream is _____ when you are hungry. (tempting, temptation)

9. We should not allow _____ to overcome us. (tempting, temptation)

10. Visual _____ can be a problem as people get older. (impairment, impaired)

11. My vision was _____ because of heavy fog. (impairment, impaired)

12. Buying a house is a good _____. (investment, investor)

13. An _____ is a person who invests money. (investment, investor)

14. Our teacher _____ us on doing a good job. (congratulated, congratulations)

15. We offered _____ to the winning team. (congratulate, congratulations)

VOCABULARY

UNIT 2 Dollars and Sense • **Lesson 5** *Business is Looking Up*

Vowel Sounds in Two-Syllable Words

Word List

1. product
2. credit
3. napkin
4. dentist
5. comment
6. cannot
7. suggest
8. within
9. glacier
10. infect
11. progress
12. topsoil
13. princess
14. rewind
15. joyful

Selection Words

16. echo
17. expert
18. bargain
19. stencil
20. predict

Pattern Study

Each syllable of a word contains a vowel sound.

▶ Break the first fifteen spelling words into syllables.

1._____   9._____

2._____   10._____

3._____   11._____

4._____   12._____

5._____   13._____

6._____   14._____

7._____   15._____

8._____

▶ Break the selection spelling words into syllables and circle the vowel sounds. Indicate whether the vowels in each word are long vowels, short vowels, or the /ə/ sound. The first one is done for you.

16. ___(e)ch•(o)___   e-short   o-long

17. _____   _____   _____

18. _____   _____   _____

19. _____   _____   _____

20. _____   _____   _____

**Vowel Sounds in
Two-Syllable Words**

SPELLING

Strategies

Proofreading Strategy Circle the misspelled
spelling words in the paragraph. Write the
correct spelling on the lines provided. There
are ten spelling errors.

The national anthem for the United States is called "The Star
Spangled Banner." Credite for writing "The Star Spangled
Banner" is given to a man named Francis Scott Key. People
surggest that Mr. Key was an ordinary man; he was not the
son of a preancess, nor was he president. "The Star Spangled
Banner" was originally written as a poem, and no one could
pridict that it would become the national anthem. Within a
few days of its publication in 1812, the prodact of Mr. Key's
pen was already being sung to the music of a familiar old
British song. The new American song proved so popular that
it was played at the Battle of New Orleans only three months
after being written. Its prograss was much slower within
government circles, however. "The Star Spangled Banner"
became the official national anthem of the United States in
1931. Today the echor of "The Star Spangled Banner" can be
heard on days such as Independence Day. However, there isn't
a day on which "The Star Spangled Banner" carnot be played.
It can be played on any occasion, joyfool or sad.

21. _____   26. _____

22. _____   27. _____

23. _____   28. _____

24. _____   29. _____

25. _____   30. _____

Review: Suffixes -*ing* and -*ly* and Base Word Families

Adding **-ly** to words creates adverbs, or words that describe the way something occurs. (swift**ly**, expert**ly**)

Adding **-ing** to verbs shows that something is happening right now. (mov**ing**)

A word that can stand alone is a base word. All the forms you can make with that word are the base word family. (spell, spell**ed**, spell**er**, spell**ing**)

Write the base word families for these words. You may use a dictionary to help you with this exercise.

1. chart _____ _____ _____ _____

2. seize _____ _____ _____ _____

3. strum _____ _____ _____ _____

4. part _____ _____ _____ _____

5. elder _____ _____ _____ _____

Practice

> **Use these words to practice using the suffixes *-ing* and *-ly* and base word families.**
>
> ▶ **chart:** a sheet that shows information in the form of a list
> ▶ **seize:** to take hold of, grab
> ▶ **strum:** to play an instrument in an easy, gentle way
> ▶ **part:** something less than the whole
> ▶ **elder:** born earlier, or older

Correct any underlined words that are used incorrectly in the sentence.

Example: As the man <u>try</u> to cross the street the light turned red. **wrong**

As the man <u>tried</u> to cross the street the light turned red. **correct**

6. <u>Uncharted</u> islands are often deserted.

_____

7. A teacher has a right to <u>seized</u> a musical instrument from a student if it is used to disrupt class.

_____

8. <u>Elder</u> people have experienced many things.

_____

9. Guitar players usually <u>strumming</u> the strings of the guitar with their fingers.

_____

10. People usually wave good-bye as they are <u>departed</u>.

_____

VOCABULARY

UNIT 2 Dollars and Sense • **Lesson 6** *Salt*

Digraphs

Word List

1. wheat
2. machine
3. couch
4. reach
5. pitch
6. leashes
7. crutches
8. author
9. cousin
10. shapeless
11. earthquake
12. stretch
13. exhaust
14. sauces
15. drawing

Selection Words

16. merchant
17. thankful
18. riches
19. minnow
20. share

Pattern Study

A **digraph** is two different letters that make one sound.

▶ Write the first ten spelling words in the column where they belong and circle the digraph in each word. Some words may belong in both columns. The first one is done for you.

Consonant Digraph	Vowel Digraph
wheat	
_____	_____
_____	_____
_____	_____
_____	_____
_____	_____
_____	_____
_____	_____
_____	_____

Digraphs • Spelling and Vocabulary Skills

UNIT 2 Dollars and Sense • **Lesson 6** *Salt*

Strategies

Visualization Strategy Rewrite the words on the lines provided and circle the vowel or consonant digraph in each word.

1. earthquake _____
2. stretch _____
3. exhaust _____
4. sauces _____
5. merchant _____
6. thankful _____
7. drawing _____
8. riches _____
9. minnow _____
10. share _____

Visualization Strategy Write three words that contain the vowel or consonant digraph in each word.

11. wheat _____ _____ _____
12. couch _____ _____ _____
13. author _____ _____ _____
14. shape _____ _____ _____
15. drawing _____ _____ _____

Review: Synonyms and Antonyms

A **synonym** is a word that is similar in meaning to another word.

An **antonym** is a word that means the opposite or almost the opposite of another word.

Write one synonym and one antonym for each word. Use a dictionary to find the meaning of the words before doing the exercise.

	Synonym	**Antonym**
1. vanished	_____	_____
2. riot	_____	_____
3. confident	_____	_____
4. rapid	_____	_____
5. firm	_____	_____

UNIT 2   Dollars and Sense • **Lesson 7** *The Milkmaid and Her Pail*

▶ **Synonyms and Antonyms**

Practice

Antonym Analogy: Front is to **back** as **left** is to **right.**

Complete the antonym analogies with an antonym from the parentheses.

   6. **Win** is to **lose** as **stop** is to _____.
      (end, start, time)

   7. **Pain** is to **pleasure** as **less** is to _____.
      (more, little, some)

   8. **End** is to **begin** as **dim** is to _____.
      (dark, shady, bright)

   9. **Much** is to **little** as **early** is to _____.
      (on time, late, right now)

 10. **Cold** is to **hot** as **cruel** is to _____.
      (lazy, helpful, kind)

Synonym Analogy: Fat is to **plump** as **large** is to **big.**

Complete the synonym analogies with one synonym from the parentheses.

 11. **Small** is to **little** as **big** is to _____.
      (tiny, large, same)

 12. **Rich** is to **wealthy** as **happy** is to _____.
      (smile, sunshine, joyful)

 13. **Take** is to **grab** as **often** is to _____.
      (frequently, not, seldom)

 14. **True** is to **loyal** as **pain** is to _____.
      (pleasure, hurt, harm)

 15. **Keep** is to **hold** as **brave** is to _____.
      (lazy, coward, courageous)

VOCABULARY

UNIT 2 Dollars and Sense • **Lesson 7** *The Milkmaid and Her Pail*

Review: The /ow/, /oi/, /er/, /âr/, and /ar/ Sounds

Word List

1. horrible
2. tower
3. plow
4. joint
5. poison
6. outside
7. destroy
8. birth
9. urgent
10. thirst
11. serve
12. library
13. narrate
14. nightmare
15. prepare

Selection Words

16. harvest
17. shower
18. pearl
19. bound
20. customer

Pattern Study

The /ow/ sound is spelled *ou* or *ow*.
The /oi/ sound is spelled *oi* or *oy*.
The /er/ sound is spelled *or, er, ear, ir,* and *ur*.
The /âr/ sound is usually spelled *are, ar, air,* or *ear*.
The /ar/ sound is usually spelled *ar*.

▶ Circle the /ow/ and /oi/ sounds in the words. Underline the /er/, /âr/, and /ar/ sounds in the words.

1. horrible
2. tower
3. plow
4. joint
5. poison
6. outside
7. destroy
8. birth
9. urgent
10. thirst
11. serve
12. library
13. narrate
14. nightmare
15. prepare
16. harvest
17. shower
18. pearl
19. bound
20. customer

UNIT 2 **Dollars and Sense • Lesson 7** *The Milkmaid and Her Pail*

 **Strategies**

The /ow/, /oi/, /er/, /âr/ and /ar/ Sounds

 Pronunciation Strategy Write five words with the /ow/ sound spelled *ou* or *ow*. The first one is done for you.

21. frown _____   24. _____

22. _____   25. _____

23. _____

Write five words with the /oi/ sound spelled *oi* or *oy*. The first one is done for you.

26. toy _____   29. _____

27. _____   30. _____

28. _____

Write five words with the /er/ sound spelled *or, er, ear, ir*, and *ur*. The first one is done for you.

31. pearl _____   34. _____

32. _____   35. _____

33. _____

Write five words with the /âr/ or /ar/ sounds. The first one is done for you.

36. share _____   39. _____

37. _____   40. _____

38. _____

SPELLING

UNIT 3   From Mystery to Medicine • **Lesson I** *Medicine: Past and Present*

Concept Words

Concept words are specific words that help you understand and discuss a certain topic. For example, if you want to understand the ideas about medicine discussed in the selection "Medicine: Past and Present," you need to know the meanings of concept words like *epidemic*, *bacteria*, *vaccine*, *sterilize*, and *immune*.

 **The following sentences contain the concept words related to medicine that are listed above. Write a definition based on context clues for each underlined word.**

1. When the Black Plague, a deadly disease, began to strike millions of people in Europe, Asia, and Africa, the people were faced with a frightening epidemic.

   epidemic: _____

2. We saw through a microscope the bacteria, or tiny living cells, that caused the disease.

   bacteria: _____

3. Pasteur developed a vaccine for the disease anthrax. This liquid, which helps the body fight off the disease, contains weakened anthrax germs.

   vaccine: _____

4. It is important to sterilize a cut with soap and water, or alcohol, to get rid of any germs.

   sterilize: _____

5. He was relieved to find that he was immune to smallpox and could not catch this dreaded disease.

   immune: _____

UNIT 3 From Mystery to Medicine • **Lesson I** *Medicine: Past and Present*

▶ Concept Words

Practice

Now that you know the meanings of these concept words from "Medicine: Past and Present," use each word in a sentence of your own. Make sure the sentence shows you know the meaning of the word.

6. epidemic: _____

_____

_____

7. bacteria: _____

_____

_____

8. vaccine: _____

_____

_____

9. sterilize: _____

_____

_____

10. immune: _____

_____

_____

VOCABULARY

The /j/ and /s/ Sounds

Word List

1. giraffe
2. generous
3. genuine
4. gentleman
5. genius
6. general
7. cymbal
8. citizen
9. cinnamon
10. certain
11. century
12. center
13. cement
14. genie
15. citrus

Selection Words

16. germs
17. generation
18. cancer
19. magical
20. circulate

Pattern Study

The /j/ sound can be spelled *ge* or *gi_*. The /s/ sound can be spelled *ce*, *ci_*, or *cy*.

▶ Write the words with the /j/ sound spelled *ge*.

1. _____   5. _____

2. _____   6. _____

3. _____   7. _____

4. _____   8. _____

▶ Write the words with the /j/ sound spelled *gi_*.

9. _____   10. _____

▶ Write the words with the /s/ sound spelled *ce*.

11. _____   14. _____

12. _____   15. _____

13. _____

▶ Write the words with the /s/ sound spelled *ci_* or *cy*.

16. _____   19. _____

17. _____   20. _____

18. _____

Name _____ Date _____

► **The /j/ and /s/ Sounds**

Strategies

Proofreading Strategy Circle the misspelled words in the following paragraphs and write the correct spellings on the lines provided.

His books have been in print for over a sentury. Jenerations of children around the world have admired his stories and poems. His works have been turned into major motion pictures. He is Rudyard Kipling, one of England's most beloved authors.

Kipling is best known for his tales about life in India and its jungles. *The Jungle Book* and *The Second Jungle Book* tell about the Indian child Mowgli who is adopted and raised by a jenerous pack of wolves after he is found alone in the jungle. The *Just So Stories* give humorous explanations about why sertain things are as they are—how the elephant got his trunk, how the rhinocerous got his skin, and how the first letters were made, for example.

Kim is jenerally regarded as Kipling's finest novel. The story senters on an Irish orphan who adopts the customs of India. Much of the novel's beauty lies in Kipling's presentation of the varying people and cultures of India. This was a subject with which Kipling was familiar, having lived and worked in India for many years.

21. _____   24. _____

22. _____   25. _____

23. _____   26. _____

SPELLING

Idioms

An idiom is a phrase or expression that has a different meaning than the literal meaning of its words. An idiom is often well known, like an old saying. For example, you may have heard the idiom "Her head was in the clouds." This statement is not meant to be taken literally and does not mean that her head is actually in the sky. It means that she is not paying attention.

Another idiom is "Peter kept his nose in a book all day." This statement does not mean that Peter's nose was actually stuck between the pages. It means that he was reading all day.

 **The following sentences contain idioms. Write what each sentence actually means.**

1. Samantha was still dead to the world at noon.

_____

2. Chin got cold feet when it was his turn to give a speech.

_____

3. We're all in the same boat.

_____

4. She's got music in her blood.

_____

5. It was a rainy day, and Steve was down in the dumps.

_____

UNIT 3 From Mystery to Medicine • **Lesson 2** *Sewed Up His Heart*

▶**Idioms**

Practice

The following sentences contain the vocabulary words below from "Sewed Up His Heart," as well as idioms. Write what each sentence actually means.

scorching: burning
sweltering: very hot
blistered: having a small bubble or swelling
tumbled: rolled or tossed about
suspended: stopped for a time

6. When he discovered he was scorching all his shirts, he asked his mother to give him a hand with the ironing.

   _____

7. I could hardly catch my breath as I jogged on that sweltering afternoon.

   _____

8. It was so hot that the sun blistered the sidewalk, and I had half a mind just to stay home.

   _____

9. The clown had the audience in stitches when he tumbled off his tricycle.

   _____

10. It was raining cats and dogs, so the game had to be suspended.

   _____

VOCABULARY

UNIT 3 From Mystery to Medicine • **Lesson 2** *Sewed Up His Heart*

The /k/ Sound

Word List

1. picnic
2. attack
3. bucket
4. check
5. frantic
6. heroic
7. lucky
8. nickel
9. picket
10. poetic
11. ticket
12. rocket
13. socket
14. plastic
15. attic

Selection Words

16. cart
17. condition
18. calm
19. tracks
20. sidewalks

Pattern Study

The /k/ sound can be spelled *k*, *c*, or *_ck*.

▶ Write the spelling word with the /k/ sound spelled *k*.

1. _____

▶ Write the spelling words with the /k/ sound spelled *c*.

2. _____   7. _____

3. _____   8. _____

4. _____   9. _____

5. _____   10. _____

6. _____

▶ Write the spelling words with the /k/ sound spelled *_ck*.

11. _____   16. _____

12. _____   17. _____

13. _____   18. _____

14. _____   19. _____

15. _____   20. _____

▶ **The /k/ Sound**

Strategies

Vowel-Substitution Strategy Replace the highlighted vowel in each spelling word with the vowels given to create new words. Write each new word on the lines after the spelling words.

21. check (*i* and *u*) _____ _____

22. picket (*a* and *o*) _____ _____

23. rocket (*a*) _____ _____

24. cart (*u*) _____ _____

25. tracks (*u* and *i*) _____ _____

Visualization Strategy Fill in the missing /k/ sound and write each word correctly on the blank.

26. pi__ni__   _____

27. atta__   _____

28. franti__   _____

29. atti__   _____

30. sidewal__s   _____

31. bu__et   _____

32. ni__el   _____

SPELLING

Metaphors

A metaphor is an original comparison between two things that are not normally compared. A metaphor says that one thing **is** another thing, rather than saying it is **like** another thing. Here are some examples of metaphors:

▶ **Peter is a clown.**

▶ **Roger's heart is an ice cube.**

▶ **We urged Rosa to finish her work, but she was a snail.**

These metaphors compare Peter to a clown, a heart to an ice cube, and Rosa to a snail. These comparisons are new and creative, and tell us something important about Peter, Roger, and Rosa. Peter is funny, Roger is not loving, and Rosa works slowly.

 **Try It!** **Describe what the writer is saying with these metaphors.**

1. At night, my room is an icebox.

_____

2. I'm a chicken when it comes to getting an injection.

_____

3. That car from the 1940s is a dinosaur.

_____

4. John's brain is a computer.

_____

5. The hat was a pancake after she sat on it.

_____

UNIT 3 From Mystery to Medicine • **Lesson 3** *The Bridge Dancers*

▶ **Metaphors**

Practice

The following metaphors contain vocabulary words from the selection "The Bridge Dancers." Write what two things are being compared in each metaphor.

6. Laura was a weak and tottery newborn lamb after being in bed for days with a terrible flu.

What two things are being compared? _____

7. Her plan was only a skeleton, but she knew it would work.

What two things are being compared? _____

8. After a night of restless sleep, her tangled hair was a jungle full of twisted vines.

What two things are being compared? _____

9. The large sailboat is a tiny toy that the rough ocean tosses.

What two things are being compared? _____

10. The creaking floorboards frightened Elizabeth with their squeaking voices.

What two things are being compared? _____

VOCABULARY

The /j/ Sound

Word List

1. badge
2. damage
3. garbage
4. image
5. manage
6. wedge
7. voyage
8. cottage
9. sausage
10. judge
11. fudge
12. cabbage
13. package
14. lodge
15. luggage

Selection Words

16. gorge
17. hedge
18. dodge
19. edge
20. bridge

Pattern Study

The /j/ sound can be spelled *ge* and *_dge*. The *_dge* spelling will usually follow a short-vowel sound, as in *badge* or *fudge*.

▶ Write the spelling words with the /j/ sound spelled *ge*.

1. _____   7. _____

2. _____   8. _____

3. _____   9. _____

4. _____   10. _____

5. _____   11. _____

6. _____

▶ Write the spelling words with the /j/ sound spelled *_dge*.

12. _____   17. _____

13. _____   18. _____

14. _____   19. _____

15. _____   20. _____

16. _____

UNIT 3 From Mystery to Medicine • **Lesson 3** *The Bridge Dancers*

▶ The /j/ Sound

Strategies

 Visualization Strategy Fill in the missing letters to write the whole spelling word.

21. gor_____   _____

22. cabba_____   _____

23. do_____   _____

24. cotta_____   _____

25. we_____   _____

26. voya_____   _____

27. bri_____   _____

28. garba_____   _____

 Family Strategy Write the spelling word that is related to each of the following words.

29. judgment   _____

30. imagine   _____

31. voyager   _____

32. lodging   _____

33. packaged   _____

SPELLING

Name _____ Date _____

Science Words

> Science words are concept words that are used to discuss and write about a variety of sciences. A scientist who studies plants may need to use science words like *chlorophyll* and *stamen*, while a scientist who studies the stars may need to use words like *dwarf* and *nebula*. Science words may seem difficult to define, but context clues can help. Here are some science words from the selection "Emily's Hands-On Science Experiment":
>
> ▶ **hypothesis:** something that is suggested as being true for the purpose of argument
>
> ▶ **experiment:** a test used to discover or prove something that involves observing results carefully
>
> ▶ **clinical:** dealing with the direct treatment of a patient rather than working in a lab
>
> ▶ **practitioner:** one who practices a profession, like a doctor
>
> ▶ **theory:** a group of ideas that explains why or how something happens

Try It! **Fill in each blank with the vocabulary word from the list above that makes sense in each sentence.**

1. The _____ was performed to test how sugar promotes tooth decay.

2. For the sake of argument, he introduced the _____ that the earthquake was not caused by a shifting of Earth's plates.

3. He is a _____ of veterinary medicine and has his own clinic.

4. Newton's _____ of gravity is the idea that what goes up must fall back down to Earth.

5. She practices _____ psychology and treats patients directly.

▶ Science Words

VOCABULARY

Practice

Use a dictionary to find the meaning of the different branches of science listed below. Write at least three words that could be used to write or speak about each type of science.

Example: geology: the study of Earth

rocks   mountains   rivers

6. entomology: the study of _____

Three words used to write about entomology: _____

_____   _____

7. astronomy: the study of _____

Three words used to write about astronomy: _____

_____   _____

8. meteorology: the study of _____

Three words used to write about meteorology: _____

_____   _____

9. zoology: the study of _____

Three words used to write about zoology: _____

_____   _____

10. botany: the study of _____

Three words used to write about botany: _____

_____   _____

The /s/ Sound

Word List

1. twice
2. surface
3. spruce
4. spice
5. prance
6. office
7. notice
8. faucet
9. process
10. distance
11. device
12. price
13. chance
14. brace
15. advice

Selection Words

16. recess
17. existence
18. conceive
19. balance
20. slice

Pattern Study

The /s/ sound can be spelled *s*, *ci_*, *ce*, or *ss*.

▶ Write the spelling words with the /s/ sound spelled *s*.

1. _____   4. _____

2. _____   5. _____

3. _____

▶ Write the spelling words with the /s/ sound spelled *ce*.

6. _____   16. _____

7. _____   17. _____

8. _____   18. _____

9. _____   19. _____

10. _____   20. _____

11. _____   21. _____

12. _____   22. _____

13. _____   23. _____

14. _____   24. _____

15. _____   25. _____

▶ Write the spelling words with the /s/ sound spelled *ss*.

26. _____   27. _____

UNIT 3 From Mystery to Medicine • **Lesson 4** *Emily's Hands-On Science Experiment*

▶ **The /s/ Sound**

Strategies

 Rhyming Strategy Write the spelling word that rhymes with each of the following words. Some words will have more than one answer.

28. dance _____ _____

29. place _____

30. mice _____ _____ _____

_____ _____ _____

31. receive _____

32. access _____ _____

33. truce _____

 Visualization Strategy Fill in the missing letters and write the whole spelling word.

34. balan___ _____

35. noti___ _____

36. exi___ten___ _____

37. con___eive _____

38. di___tan___ _____

39. chan___ _____

40. re___e___ _____

SPELLING

UNIT 3 From Mystery to Medicine • **Lesson 5** *The New Doctor*

Spanish Words

As you read stories like the one told in the selection "The New Doctor," you may come across words from different languages, such as Spanish. These words help make the story more realistic by showing how the characters actually speak. You may not know the meanings of these words unless you speak that language yourself. But you can try to figure out the meanings from context clues.

Before you can discover the meanings of Spanish words, you must learn to recognize them in the texts you read. Spanish words frequently end with the vowels *a* or *o*. Here are some Spanish words from "The New Doctor":

▶ **fiesta:** a party

▶ **curandera:** a healer who uses remedies such as herbs

▶ **tortilla:** a thin, round, flat bread made with flour

▶ **amigo:** a friend

▶ **mesa:** a hill or mountain with a flat top and steep sides

Try It! **Fill in each blank with the Spanish word from the list above that makes sense in the sentence.**

1. We stood on top of the _____ and looked across the desert.

2. The _____ lasted until two o'clock in the morning, when the last of the guests finally went home.

3. When he was feeling ill, he went to see the _____, who gave him some willow-bark tea.

4. My parents said I could choose one _____ to invite to the zoo.

5. Lupe wrapped cheese and beans inside a large _____.

Practice

Now that you know the meanings of the Spanish words listed on the previous page, use each one in a sentence of your own. Be creative and make sure the sentence shows that you know the meaning of the word.

6. fiesta: _____

_____

_____

7. curandera: _____

_____

_____

8. tortilla: _____

_____

_____

9. amigo: _____

_____

_____

10. mesa: _____

_____

_____

VOCABULARY

UNIT 3 From Mystery to Medicine • **Lesson 5** *The New Doctor*

The /ch/ Sound

Word List

1. wrench
2. watch
3. twitch
4. sketch
5. pinch
6. branch
7. church
8. clutch
9. fetch
10. scratch
11. splotch
12. starch
13. torch
14. stretch
15. reach

Selection Words

16. screech
17. chatter
18. perch
19. hopscotch
20. cheek

Pattern Study

The /ch/ sound is spelled *ch* or *_tch*. If the /ch/ sound is at the beginning of a word, it is spelled *ch*. The /ch/ sound is often spelled *_tch* at the end of a word, after a short vowel, as in *latch*.

▶ Write the spelling words with the /ch/ sound spelled *_tch*.

1. _____ 6. _____

2. _____ 7. _____

3. _____ 8. _____

4. _____ 9. _____

5. _____

▶ Write the spelling words with the /ch/ sound spelled *ch*.

10. _____ 16. _____

11. _____ 17. _____

12. _____ 18. _____

13. _____ 19. _____

14. _____ 20. _____

15. _____

UNIT 3 From Mystery to Medicine • **Lesson 5** *The New Doctor*

The /ch/ Sound

Strategies

Visualization Strategy **Circle the correct spelling for each word and write it in the blank.**

21. screech   screash   screeche   _____

22. wrensh   wrenche   wrench   _____

23. pertch   perch   percth   _____

24. hopscotch   hopscoch   hopscotsh   _____

25. stretch   strech   stretsh   _____

26. wauch   watch   wach   _____

27. churtch   shurch   church   _____

28. fetsh   fetch   fech   _____

Vowel-Substitution Strategy **Write the spelling word that is created by adding, dropping, or substituting one or more vowel sounds.**

29. splutch   _____

30. bronch   _____

31. wrinch   _____

32. reech   _____

33. fitch   _____

34. porch   _____

35. twutch   _____

SPELLING

Concept Words

You will remember that concept words are words that are used to write about or understand a certain subject. The selection "The Story of Susan La Flesche Picotte" contains a number of concept words used to describe the experience of Susan La Flesche Picotte, the first female Native American doctor in the United States.

 **Try It!** Write a definition for the underlined word based on context clues.

1. The valley was <u>inundated</u> with rain day after day; it was so overwhelmed that its rivers began to flood.

What does inundated mean? _____

_____

2. She endured a <u>siege</u> of illnesses and was attacked constantly by colds, flus, and viruses.

What does siege mean? _____

_____

3. He discovered that he was suffering from the <u>grippe</u>, a flu-like disease that could be spread to others.

What does grippe mean? _____

_____

4. The doctor said that the reason I felt so ill and had trouble breathing was because my lungs were infected with <u>pneumonia</u>.

What is pneumonia? _____

_____

Practice

Now that you know the meanings of the vocabulary words on the previous page, use each one in a sentence of your own. Make sure your sentence shows that you know the meaning of the word.

5. inundated: _____

_____

_____

6. siege: _____

_____

_____

7. grippe: _____

_____

_____

8. pneumonia: _____

_____

_____

VOCABULARY

The /sh/ Sound

Word List

1. shawl
2. attention
3. shelter
4. education
5. information
6. shatter
7. addition
8. publish
9. ambitious
10. shoulder
11. social
12. special
13. delicious
14. official
15. ancient

Selection Words

16. physician
17. vicious
18. instruction
19. directions
20. accomplish

Pattern Study

The /sh/ sound can be spelled *sh*, *_ci_*, or *_ti_*. The /sh/ sound can be spelled *_ci_* when followed by the endings **-ous, -al, -an,** or **-ent.** The /sh/ sound can be spelled *_ti_* in the ending **-tion** and before the ending **-ous.**

▶ Write the spelling words with the /sh/ sound spelled *sh.*

1. _____   4. _____

2. _____   5. _____

3. _____   6. _____

▶ Write the spelling words with the /sh/ sound spelled *_ci_.*

7. _____   11. _____

8. _____   12. _____

9. _____   13. _____

10. _____

▶ Write the spelling words with the /sh/ sound spelled *_ti_.*

14. _____   18. _____

15. _____   19. _____

16. _____   20. _____

17. _____

▶**The /sh/ Sound**

SPELLING

Strategies

Meaning Strategy Choose the word that best completes each sentence.

21. We learn _____ in math class.
(addition, added)

22. A dinner party is a _____ event.
(socialize, social)

23. People who are _____ want to succeed.
(ambitious, ambition)

24. Fresh cookies are always _____.
(deliciously, delicious)

25. The pyramids of Egypt are _____.
(ancient, anciently)

26. A _____ can treat many illnesses.
(physician, physicians)

27. We go to school to gain an _____.
(educate, education)

28. There is a homeless _____ in almost every
city. (shelter, sheltered)

29. A _____ can keep your shoulders from
getting cold. (shawl, shawls)

30. I _____ the plate by dropping it on the floor.
(shatter, shattered)

Metaphors

> As you learned earlier in this unit, a **metaphor** is an original comparison between two things that are not normally compared. A metaphor says that one thing **is** another thing, rather than saying it is **like** another thing.
>
> A **simile** is a comparison that is similar to a metaphor, but uses the words *like* or *as*. A simile is also a creative comparison that helps describe something; it is stated in a different way.
>
> ▶ **Metaphor:** His stomach is a bottomless pit.
> ▶ **Simile:** His stomach is **like** a bottomless pit.
>
> ▶ **Metaphor:** The clouds were fluffy clumps of cotton candy.
> ▶ **Simile:** The clouds were **as** fluffy **as** cotton candy.

 **Write whether each sentence contains a metaphor or a simile. Then write what two things are being compared.**

1. The newly washed towel was as white as snow. _____

   What two things are being compared? _____

2. Dad was a busy bee and spent his entire Saturday afternoon in the garage

   working on the car. _____

   What two things are being compared? _____

3. Joe is the glue that holds our team together. _____

   What two things are being compared? _____

4. When we pulled the shades, the room was dark as night. _____

   What two things are being compared? _____

5. The stars were bright eyes winking at us. _____

   What two things are being compared? _____

UNIT 3 From Mystery to Medicine • **Lesson 7** *Shadow of a Bull*

▶ **Metaphors**

Practice

The following metaphors contain these vocabulary words from "Shadow of a Bull." Write what two things are being compared after each metaphor.

gored: pierced or wounded by something pointed, like a horn or knife
carved: cut carefully into a shape
shuffled: walked by dragging the feet
ammonia: a colorless liquid with a strong smell that can be used as a cleaner
invaded: spread over or entered in order to take over

6. The bull's horn was a sharp knife as it gored the bullfighter.

   What two things are being compared? _____

7. A sea of wood shavings covered the porch as grandfather sat and carved wooden canes.

   What two things are being compared? _____

8. An endless parade of students shuffled into the lunchroom.

   What two things are being compared? _____

9. The ammonia was a powerful fighter and killed the germs on the dirty kitchen floor.

   What two things are being compared? _____

10. An army of birds invaded the feeder and pecked at the birdseed for hours.

    What two things are being compared? _____

VOCABULARY

Review: /j/, /s/, /k/, /ch/ Sounds

Word List

1. generous
2. general
3. century
4. check
5. nickel
6. heroic
7. judge
8. manage
9. image
10. twice
11. spruce
12. advice
13. watch
14. scratch
15. branch

Selection Words

16. gesture
17. gently
18. pieces
19. touching
20. dangerous

Pattern Study

These spelling words review the /j/, /s/, /k/, and /ch/ sounds.

▶ Write the spelling words with the /j/ sound spelled *ge* or *_dge*.

1. _____   5. _____

2. _____   6. _____

3. _____   7. _____

4. _____   8. _____

▶ Write the spelling words with the /s/ sound spelled *ci_* or *ce*.

9. _____   12. _____

10. _____   13. _____

11. _____

▶ Write the spelling words with the /k/ sound spelled *k*, *_ck*, or *c*.

14. _____   16. _____

15. _____   17. _____

▶ Write four spelling words with the /ch/ sound spelled *ch* or *_tch*.

18. _____   20. _____

19. _____   21. _____

▶ **The /j/, /s/, /k/, and /ch/ Sounds**

Strategies

Consonant-Substitution Strategy Write the spelling word that is made when the highlighted consonants are changed.

22. **sp**eck _____

23. **f**udge _____

24. **sp**ice _____

25. **h**atch _____

Visualization Strategy Circle the words that are spelled correctly.

26. totching   touching   toushing

27. dangerous   danjerous   dangrous

28. jeography   gography   geography

29. jeneral   gineral   general

30. century   sentury   ceantury

31. advyse   advice   advic

32. scratch   scrach   scratsh

SPELLING

UNIT 4 Survival • Lesson I *Island of the Blue Dolphins*

Word Origins

Many words have been shortened by common usage. Often it is more convenient, and more informal, to use a shortened version of a long word.

▶ **telephone:** used to make calls

▶ **luncheon:** a formal lunch

▶ **automobile:** a car or other motor vehicle

▶ **refrigerator:** used to keep food cold

▶ **limousine:** a large vehicle or car often driven by a chauffeur

 **Try It!** **Circle the shortened form of the vocabulary word in each sentence. Then write the long form of each word on the lines provided.**

1. After the phone rang twice my brother answered it.

_____

2. We eat lunch at noon. _____

3. An auto is a car. _____

4. The drinks in the fridge are cold. _____

5. The bride and groom rode in a limo. _____

UNIT 4 Survival • **Lesson I** *Island of the Blue Dolphins*

▶ Word Origins

Practice

Use the shortened form of each underlined word in a sentence of your own. If you need to, use a dictionary to help you complete this activity. The first one is done for you.

6. The SAT is an <u>examination</u> given to students in grade twelve.

I had an *exam* last week. _____

7. Some offices have an employee <u>luncheon</u> once a year.

_____

8. The <u>gymnasium</u> was crowded during the basketball game.

_____

9. People with <u>influenza</u> may have a fever and a cough.

_____

10. The man took a <u>photograph</u> of a lion at the zoo.

_____

11. Most cars need <u>gasoline</u> to run.

_____

12. We rode in a <u>taxicab</u> because our car wasn't running.

_____

13. A pilot is a person who flies an <u>airplane</u>.

_____

14. Another name for trousers is <u>pantaloons</u>.

_____

VOCABULARY

UNIT 4 Survival • **Lesson I** *Island of the Blue Dolphins*

Plurals

Word List

1. tomatoes
2. countries
3. dollars
4. eagles
5. inches
6. leashes
7. monkeys
8. numbers
9. smudges
10. taxes
11. relishes
12. sandwiches
13. umbrellas
14. bicycles
15. ferries

Selection Words

16. arrows
17. ages
18. times
19. tides
20. cliffs

Pattern Study

Plurals name more than one person, place, or thing.

▶ Write the spelling words to which *s* was added to create plurals.

1. _____   7. _____

2. _____   8. _____

3. _____   9. _____

4. _____   10. _____

5. _____   11. _____

6. _____   12. _____

▶ Write the spelling words to which the *y* ending has been changed to *ies* to create plurals.

13. _____   14. _____

▶ Write the words ending in *ch*, *sh*, *o*, and *x* to which *es* has been added to create plurals.

15. _____   18. _____

16. _____   19. _____

17. _____   20. _____

UNIT 4 Survival • **Lesson 1** *Island of the Blue Dolphins*

▶ Plurals

SPELLING

Strategies

Conventions Strategy Write the singular form of the following words. Then write its plural ending (*es*, *ies*, *s*). The first one is done for you.

21. tomatoes   *tomato*   *es*

22. countries   _____   _____

23. dollars   _____   _____

24. eagles   _____   _____

25. inches   _____   _____

26. leashes   _____   _____

27. monkeys   _____   _____

28. numbers   _____   _____

29. smudges   _____   _____

30. taxes   _____   _____

31. relishes   _____   _____

Conventions Strategy Not all plurals follow the *s*, *es*, and *ies* patterns. Write the plural form of the underlined word on the line provided.

32. The <u>man</u> was one of many _____ in the room.

33. The <u>woman</u> made earrings for _____.

34. The <u>goose</u> did not play with the other _____.

35. Twelve inches equals one <u>foot</u>, and one yard equals three

_____.

UNIT 4 Survival • **Lesson 2** *Arctic Explorer: The Story of Matthew Henson*

Hyphenated Compound Words

Many compound words are **hyphenated compound words.**

You can use a dictionary to learn if a compound word is hyphenated.

first-class   **well-done**

Many numbers are also hyphenated compound words.

forty-five   **seventy-six**

 **Try It!** **Read each set of sentences and circle the correct compound word.**

1. There was a sweet-smelling scent coming from the bakery.
   Garbage does not have a sweet-smelling-scent.

2. Karate is a form of self-defense.
   Not all self defense-classes teach you karate.

3. A polar bear is a-warm blooded-animal.
   Mammals and birds are warm-blooded.

4. Lumberjacks use chainsaws to get clean-cut wood.
   Something that is cleancut has a smooth edge.

5. We usually go to parties emptyhanded.
   We should never go to school empty-handed.

► **Hyphenated Compound Words**

Practice

**Read each sentence below and write an explanation
for each underlined word. You may use a dictionary
if you need help.**

6. When I hurt myself, it took a lot of <u>self-control</u> to
keep from crying.

_____

7. Because my sister refused to help me, I
<u>single-handedly</u> cleaned out the garage.

_____

_____

8. Mother gave me <u>step-by-step</u> instructions on how to
bake biscuits.

_____

_____

9. I had to <u>lip-read</u> his words because he spoke in a very
soft voice.

_____

_____

10. Martha <u>baby-sits</u> my baby brother when my parents
go out dancing.

_____

_____

VOCABULARY

UNIT 4 Survival • **Lesson 2** *Arctic Explorer: The Story of Matthew Henson*

Compound Words

Word List

1. goldfish
2. fireplace
3. brainstorm
4. earthquake
5. lifeguard
6. footprint
7. grapevine
8. headache
9. bathroom
10. pigpen
11. sometimes
12. spotlight
13. waterfall
14. newspaper
15. billboard

Selection Words

16. outfit
17. handshake
18. moonlight
19. lifetime
20. understand

Pattern Study

Compound words are words made of two or more smaller words.

▶ Break each compound word into two smaller words.

1. _____ 11. _____
2. _____ 12. _____
3. _____ 13. _____
4. _____ 14. _____
5. _____ 15. _____
6. _____ 16. _____
7. _____ 17. _____
8. _____ 18. _____
9. _____ 19. _____
10. _____ 20. _____

▶ **Compound Words**

SPELLING

Strategies

Compound Word Strategy Use the two smaller words that make up the compound word to write the meaning of the compound word. Use a dictionary to find the meanings of words you do not know. The first one is done for you.

21. goldfish   *a fish that's gold* _____

22. fireplace   _____

23. earthquake   _____

24. lifeguard   _____

25. footprint   _____

26. bathroom   _____

27. sometimes   _____

28. newspaper   _____

29. waterfall   _____

30. moonlight   _____

31. handshake   _____

32. headache   _____

Meaning Strategy Complete each sentence with one of the spelling words.

33. Grapes grow on a _____.

34. Pigs live in a _____.

35. A sudden bright idea is a _____.

UNIT 4 Survival • **Lesson 3** *McBroom and the Big Wind*

Personification

Writers use **personification** to give a human quality to things that aren't human. Adding personification to our work makes our writing come alive. Here is an example of personification:

I listened to the leaves whispering in the wind.

 **Circle the words or phrases that create personification in the sentences.**

1. The cereal had a sad look after it had been left in milk all day.

2. The bush cried for mercy as the girl stomped on it with her hiking boots.

3. The floor smiled brightly after the scrubbing I gave it.

4. The door winced in pain as we pounded on it.

5. The flower danced in the wind.

UNIT 4 Survival • **Lesson 3** *McBroom and the Big Wind*

▶**Personification**

VOCABULARY

Write the meaning of each sentence on the line provided.

6. Just last year a blow came ripping across our farm and carried off a pail of sweet milk.

_____

7. My birthday cake shouted, "Eat me! Eat me!"

_____

8. The sun went back to bed early in the day.

_____

9. I didn't want the wind picking them up by the ears.

_____

10. The tree had a gaping wound after the man swung an axe at it.

_____

11. Our farm was watered with tears from the sky.

_____

12. The thieving wind was apt to make off with our rich topsoil.

_____

13. Finally the wind gave up butting its fool head against the door.

_____

UNIT 4 Survival • **Lesson 3** *McBroom and the Big Wind*

Abbreviations

Word List

1. Aug.
2. Ave.
3. Blvd.
4. Dec.
5. Fri.
6. Sun.
7. Mon.
8. Tues.
9. Wed.
10. Thurs.
11. Sat.
12. Sept.
13. Mar.
14. Nov.
15. Oct.

Selection Words

16. Apr.
17. Feb.
18. Jan.
19. Rd.
20. St.

Pattern Study

An **abbreviation** is a group of letters that stands for a longer word or phrase.

▶ Write the abbreviations for the days of the week.

1. _____   5. _____

2. _____   6. _____

3. _____   7. _____

4. _____

▶ Write the abbreviations for the months of the year.

8. _____   13. _____

9. _____   14. _____

10. _____   15. _____

11. _____   16. _____

12. _____

▶ Write the abbreviations for street names.

17. _____   19. _____

18. _____   20. _____

UNIT 4 Survival • **Lesson 3** *McBroom and the Big Wind*

▶**Abbreviations**

Strategies

Dictionary Strategy **Write the meaning for each abbreviation.**

21. The president lives on Pennsylvania Ave. in

    Washington, D.C. _____

22. Anton lives on Oakwood Blvd. _____

23. Dec. is the last month of the year. _____

24. The school week ends on Fri. _____

25. The week begins on Sun. _____

Visualization Strategy **Write the abbreviation for each underlined word.**

26. Most people go to work on Monday. _____

27. Labor Day is in September. _____

28. Thanksgiving is in November. _____

29. The first month of the year is January. _____

30. February is the shortest month of the year. _____

SPELLING

UNIT 4 Survival • **Lesson 4** *The Big Wave*

Latin Roots

Many **Latin roots** can be found in the English language. Recognizing and knowing Latin roots can help you discover word meanings. The Latin root *form* means "shape."

Use the vocabulary words to practice identifying latin roots.

▶ **platform:** a raised surface

▶ **uniform:** having the same form as others

▶ **transform:** to change in appearance

▶ **reform:** to make or change for the better

▶ **inform:** to tell

 **Try It!** **Circle the root in each word.**

1. platform

2. uniform

3. transform

4. reform

5. inform

Use each word in a sentence.

6. platform: _____

7. uniform: _____

8. transform: _____

9. reform: _____

10. inform: _____

UNIT 4 Survival • **Lesson 4** *The Big Wave*

▶**Latin Roots**

Practice

Circle the Latin root in each word. Use a dictionary to write the meaning of each word.

11. sensation _____

_____

12. sense _____

_____

13. sensitive _____

_____

14. sensible _____

_____

15. sensory _____

_____

16. vacant _____

_____

17. vacation _____

_____

18. vacuum _____

_____

19. evacuate _____

_____

20. vacate _____

_____

VOCABULARY

UNIT 4 Survival • **Lesson 4** *The Big Wave*

Doubling Final Consonants

Word List

1. drag
2. drip
3. star
4. thin
5. knot
6. quit
7. snap
8. scar
9. knit
10. plug
11. tug
12. mop
13. rip
14. chop
15. hiss

Selection Words

16. shopping
17. sobbing
18. clapping
19. petting
20. begged

Pattern Study

Final consonants are often doubled when suffixes are added to a word.

▶ Add *-ing* or *-ed* to each spelling word.

1. _____   9. _____

2. _____   10. _____

3. _____   11. _____

4. _____   12. _____

5. _____   13. _____

6. _____   14. _____

7. _____   15. _____

8. _____

▶ Write the base word for each selection word.

16. _____

17. _____

18. _____

19. _____

20. _____

▶**Doubling Final Consonants**

Strategies

Conventions Strategy Circle the sentence in which the underlined word is used incorrectly. Rewrite the sentence using the underlined word correctly.

Example:
The faucet <u>dripped</u> all night long.
⟨The faucet <u>dripping</u> all night long.⟩

The faucet was dripping all night long.

21. The old man has <u>thinning</u> hair.
    The old man has <u>thinned</u> hair.

    _____

22. Her left leg <u>scarring</u> after healing.
    Her left leg <u>scarred</u> after healing.

    _____

23. My family and I will go <u>shopping</u> today.
    My family and I will go <u>shopped</u> today.

    _____

24. My father <u>mopped</u> the floor yesterday.
    My father <u>mopping</u> the floor yesterday.

    _____

25. The audience <u>clapping</u> after the play was over.
    The audience <u>clapped</u> after the play was over.

    _____

SPELLING

UNIT 4 Survival • **Lesson 5** *Anne Frank: The Diary of a Young Girl*

Homophones

Homophones are words that have the same sound but different meanings.

Most people **write** with their **right** hand.

Knowing the meaning of a word is very important when using homophones. If you do not know the meaning of a homophone, you could use the word incorrectly.

Most people **right** with their **write** hand. (wrong)

 **Try It!** Complete each sentence with the correct homophone.

> **sole   soul**

1. A person who helps others has a kind _____.

2. The bottom part of your foot is the _____.

> **rain   reign**

3. Water that falls from the sky is called _____.

4. The people lived in peace under the _____ of a new king.

> **stares   stairs**

5. The bright red float got many _____ during the parade.

6. I climbed the _____ slowly.

UNIT 4 Survival • **Lesson 5** *Anne Frank: The Diary of a Young Girl*

▶ **Homophones**

Practice

tale	rode	weigh	flower	fare
tail	road	way	flour	fair
plane	piece			
plain	peace			

Complete each sentence or phrase with a homophone from the box.

7. Sally wore a _____ dress.

8. The _____ landed smoothly.

9. I had a _____ of cake for dessert.

10. The police department keeps the _____.

11. We use _____ to bake bread.

12. Roses are my favorite type of _____.

13. Our dog wags her _____ when she sees us coming home.

14. The captain of the ship told us a _____ about life at sea.

15. One _____ to paint the ceiling is to stand on a ladder.

16. How much do you _____?

17. The judges were _____ in awarding prizes.

18. The cost of riding on a bus or train is called the _____.

19. I _____ a donkey at the zoo.

20. The _____ was slippery after the ice storm.

VOCABULARY

UNIT 4 Survival • **Lesson 5** *Anne Frank: The Diary of a Young Girl*

Changing y to i

Word List

1. happy
2. stormy
3. heavy
4. dirty
5. frosty
6. hungry
7. mighty
8. naughty
9. angry
10. windy
11. merry
12. bumpy
13. crazy
14. thirsty
15. speedy

Selection Words

16. grouchy
17. stingy
18. sturdy
19. steady
20. clumsy

Pattern Study

For words ending in consonant *y*, the letter *y* is usually changed to *i* when adding endings such as *-er*.

▶ Add the ending *-er* to each spelling word.

1. _____   11. _____

2. _____   12. _____

3. _____   13. _____

4. _____   14. _____

5. _____   15. _____

6. _____   16. _____

7. _____   17. _____

8. _____   18. _____

9. _____   19. _____

10. _____   20. _____

UNIT 4 Survival • **Lesson 5** *Anne Frank: The Diary of a Young Girl*

► **Changing *y* to *i***

Strategies

Family Strategy Write the base word for each base word family. The first one is done for you.

21. happier	happiest	happily	*happy*
22. merrier	merriest	merrily	_____
23. heavier	heaviest	heavily	_____
24. dirty	dirtier	dirtiest	_____
25. crazier	craziest	crazily	_____
26. hungrier	hungriest	hungrily	_____
27. stingier	stingiest	stingily	_____
28. angrier	angriest	angrily	_____
29. stormier	stormiest	stormy	_____
30. naughtier	naughtiest	naughtiness	_____

SPELLING

UNIT 4 Survival • **Lesson 6** *Music and Slavery*

Homophones and Personification

> **Homophones** are words that sound the same but have different spellings and meanings.
>
> Soldiers in the army **wear** the same uniforms.
>
> **Where** are the new uniforms we bought yesterday?
>
> **Personification** means giving human qualities to things that aren't human.

 **Fill in the blanks with the correct homophone from the parentheses.**

1. Are _____ bookbags in here or over _____? (their, there)

2. Have you _____ that book with the _____ cover? (red, read)

3. We heard him _____ as the _____ moved next to him in the water. (whale, wail)

4. The _____ to enter the _____ was very expensive. (fare, fair)

5. I _____ the _____ of elephants moving around as I walked through the forest. (herd, heard)

Circle the words or phrases that create personification in the sentences.

6. The wind whistled through the trees.

7. The leaves danced in the breeze.

8. The angry volcano spat out hot molten lava.

UNIT 4 Survival • **Lesson 6** *Music and Slavery*

Homophones and Personification

Practice

Circle the words or phrases that create personification in the sentences.

9. The sun smiled on us.

10. Finally about midmorning, the wind got tired of blowing one way, so it blew the other.

11. The house creaked and trembled.

12. With a great angry sigh the wind turned and whisked itself away.

13. The sky was turning dark and mean.

14. The wind plucked that turkey clean, pinfeathers and all.

15. The ball cried for help when it was tossed against the wall.

Fill in the blanks with the correct homophone from the parentheses.

16. She _____ that our _____ would arrive late. (guessed, guest)

17. I've _____ the last _____ of that movie three times. (scene, seen)

18. If you _____ here for a moment, Travis will check your _____. (weight, wait)

19. The _____ at the zoo sat on the

    _____ ground. (bear, bare)

20. We are not _____ to read _____ in the library. (aloud, allowed)

VOCABULARY

UNIT 4 Survival • **Lesson 6** *Music and Slavery*

Abbreviations and Plurals

Word List

1. Aug.
2. Ave.
3. Blvd.
4. Dec.
5. Fri.
6. Sun.
7. Mon.
8. mo.
9. wk.
10. yr.
11. tomatoes
12. countries
13. dollars
14. eagles
15. inches

Selection Words

16. leashes
17. monkeys
18. numbers
19. hours
20. cabins

Pattern Study

Use the words provided to review **abbreviations** and **plurals.**

▶ Write the words to which *s*, *-es*, or *-ies* was added to form a plural. The first one is done for you.

1. tomato _____   6. _____
2. _____   7. _____
3. _____   8. _____
4. _____   9. _____
5. _____   10. _____

▶ Write the meaning of each abbreviation listed.

11. _____   16. _____
12. _____   17. _____
13. _____   18. _____
14. _____   19. _____
15. _____   20. _____

UNIT 4 Survival • **Lesson 6** *Music and Slavery*

▶ Abbreviations and Plurals

Strategies

Proofreading Strategy Circle the plurals that are spelled incorrectly in the paragraph. Write the correct form of the words on the lines provided.

Different types of foods are grown on each farm. Some farmers grow vegetablies such as tomatos and corn, and other farmers raise animales such as chickenes. Farmers who grow vegetables spend many hours plowing their land before growing their cropies. Farmers who raise animals spend a lot of time feeding their animals. You will find different typies of animals on an animal farm. You may find cows, pigies, and chickens. Monkeyes and eaglies aren't usually raised on a farm. Most farmers sell their products for money. Vegetables and animals bring lots of dollares to farmers.

Farming isn't a profession for everyone. Some people don't enjoy farming, but there are people who do. If you choose to be a farmer, you will have to work hard.

21. _____ 26. _____

22. _____ 27. _____

23. _____ 28. _____

24. _____ 29. _____

25. _____ 30. _____

RECYCLE!
THE EARTH NEEDS YOU!

SPELLING

Name _____ Date _____

Descriptive Words

Descriptive words are adjectives that are used to describe a person, place, thing, or idea.

Vocabulary Words

▶ **severe:** very strict or harsh

▶ **shrill:** having a sharp or high sound

▶ **thick:** having much space between one side of something and another; not thin

▶ **rusty:** covered with rust

▶ **throbbing:** beating or pounding heavily or fast

 **Try It!**

Use each descriptive word in a sentence.

1. severe _____

_____

2. shrill _____

_____

3. thick _____

_____

4. rusty _____

_____

5. throbbing _____

_____

UNIT 5 Communication • **Lesson I** *Messages by the Mile*

▶**Descriptive Words**

VOCABULARY

Practice

Circle the descriptive word in the sentence. Write the meaning of the word on the lines provided.

6. The telephone was invented by a clever man named

Alexander Graham Bell. _____

_____

7. Mr. Bell was a marvelous student who graduated from

high school at age 14. _____

_____

8. Mr. Bell was a young man when he invented the

telephone; he was only 29 years old. _____

_____

9. The telegraph was used to send urgent messages.

_____

10. The telephone is an important machine, used to

communicate messages. _____

_____

11. The telephone is an improvement on the telegraph,

because it is faster. _____

_____

12. Mr. Bell did not have skillful hands. _____

_____

UNIT 5 Communication • **Lesson 1** *Messages by the Mile*

Words with *re-* or *un-*

Word List

1. rearrange
2. redo
3. remove
4. renew
5. replace
6. reverse
7. review
8. unbeaten
9. unequal
10. unfair
11. unfinished
12. unfit
13. uncover
14. unplanned
15. report

Selection Words

16. repackage
17. recount
18. untamed
19. rewrite
20. recall

Pattern Study

> The prefix *re-* means "again."
> The prefix *un-* means "not."

▶ Remove the prefix *re-* from the words to create a base word. The first one is done for you.

1. arrange   7. _____
2. _____   8. _____
3. _____   9. _____
4. _____   10. _____
5. _____   11. _____
6. _____   12. _____

▶ Remove the prefix *un-* from the word to create a base word. The first one is done for you.

13. beaten   17. _____
14. _____   18. _____
15. _____   19. _____
16. _____   20. _____

UNIT 5 Communication • **Lesson 1** *Messages by the Mile*

▶ **Words with *re-* or *un-***

Strategies

Family Strategy Write the base word for each base word family. The first one is done for you.

21. unfair fairly fairer fairest _____*fair*_____

22. rewrite rewriting writing written _____

23. recall recalling called calling _____

24. untamed tamed taming tamer _____

25. recount recounted counting counted _____

Meaning Strategy The prefix *re-* means "again." The prefix *un-* means "not." Write the meanings of the spelling words, using the base word and the meaning of the prefix. The first one is done for you.

26. renew *To make new again*_____

27. unequal _____

28. unfit _____

29. untamed _____

30. rewrite _____

UNIT 5 Communication • **Lesson 2** *We'll Be Right Back After These Messages*

Multiple Meanings

Many words have more than one meaning.
A **bat** is a small furry animal that flies.
A **bat** is a stick or club used to hit a baseball.

Vocabulary Words

▶ **watch:** to look at a person or thing carefully

▶ **brand:** a kind or make of something

▶ **prime:** of the best quality, excellent

▶ **boom:** increase dramatically

▶ **press:** magazines, newspapers

Try It!

Write the vocabulary word that fits each description.

1. A device worn on your wrist to tell time: _____

2. My favorite pair of tennis shoes has a _____ name.

3. First or greatest in importance or value: _____

4. A deep, hollow sound: _____

5. To push something: _____

UNIT 5 Communication • **Lesson 2** *We'll Be Right Back After These Messages*

▶ **Multiple Meanings**

Practice

fan	play	groom	hit

Complete each sentence with a word from the box.

6. The drama club is producing a _____.

7. We should never _____ each other.

8. I _____ baseball on weekends.

9. We turn on the _____ when the weather is warm.

10. I'm a big _____ of action movies.

11. The _____ was a hit.

12. The _____ was late for his wedding.

Write two meanings for the word *runs* used in the sentence.

Tracy **runs** for class president.

13. _____

14. _____

VOCABULARY

UNIT 5 Communication • **Lesson 2** *We'll Be Right Back After These Messages*

Words with -tion, -ture, or -ure

Word List

1. motion
2. protection
3. measure
4. construction
5. mixture
6. creation
7. location
8. condition
9. furniture
10. lecture
11. moisture
12. nature
13. failure
14. question
15. picture

Selection Words

16. situation
17. pleasure
18. action
19. introduction
20. departure

Pattern Study

If a word ends in a vowel, the vowel is dropped before the *-tion* ending is added, as in *introduce, introduction*.

▶ Write the spelling words with the suffix *-tion*.

1. _____   6. _____

2. _____   7. _____

3. _____   8. _____

4. _____   9. _____

5. _____   10. _____

▶ Write the spelling words with the suffix *-ture*.

11. _____   15. _____

12. _____   16. _____

13. _____   17. _____

14. _____

▶ Write the spelling words with the suffix *-ure*.

18. _____   20. _____

19. _____

UNIT 5 Communication • **Lesson 2** *We'll Be Right Back After These Messages*

Strategies

▶ **Words with *-tion, -ture,* or *-ure***

 Proofreading Strategy **Circle the misspelled word in the sentence and write the correct spelling on the line provided.**

21. Construcshon workers build many things. _____

22. Batter is a mixtur used to make pancakes. _____

23. Their new house is in a beautiful locatione on top of the hill.

_____

24. We can keep in good condion by exercising. _____

25. Teachers usually lectore to their students. _____

26. In some places there is moitrue on the grass during the morning.

_____

27. Plants and animals are a part of natore. _____

28. I was disappointed at the failore of the plant to grow. _____

29. We use a camera to take a pictuore. _____

30. The process of doing something is called acshion. _____

SPELLING

Derivations

> **Derivations** are words that are derived from, or come from, other languages. The word *vitamin* comes from a Latin word meaning "life."
>
> **Use the vocabulary words to practice derivations.**
> ▶ **nostril:** derived from Latin meaning "nose and hole"
> ▶ **fluid:** derived from Latin meaning "to flow"
> ▶ **language:** derived from Latin meaning "tongue"
> ▶ **biscuit:** derived from French meaning "baked dough"
> ▶ **glossary:** derived from Latin meaning "dictionary"

Replace the underlined parts of the sentence with one of the vocabulary words.

1. It's hard for me to breathe through my <u>nose</u> when I have

   a cold. _____

2. There was <u>water flowing</u> in the sink. _____

3. The man spoke a foreign <u>tongue</u>. _____

4. For lunch we had <u>baked dough</u> and jam. _____

5. I found the definition of the word in the <u>dictionary</u>.

   _____

Practice

The names of the following states were taken from other languages. Write the language and the definition from which the names of the states are derived. Use a dictionary to complete this exercise.

6. Colorado _____

_____

7. Alabama _____

_____

8. Wyoming _____

_____

9. Tennessee _____

_____

10. South Dakota _____

_____

11. Nevada _____

_____

12. Nebraska _____

_____

13. Indiana _____

_____

14. Florida _____

_____

VOCABULARY

Words with -ly

Word List

1. secretly
2. badly
3. barely
4. certainly
5. suddenly
6. kindly
7. lately
8. loyally
9. gladly
10. loudly
11. quietly
12. proudly
13. likely
14. finally
15. deeply

Selection Words

16. closely
17. boldly
18. rarely
19. costly
20. quickly

Pattern Study

The suffix **-ly** can be added to a word without dropping the final *e* or doubling the final consonant.

▶ Drop the suffix **-ly** from each word.

1. _____   11. _____
2. _____   12. _____
3. _____   13. _____
4. _____   14. _____
5. _____   15. _____
6. _____   16. _____
7. _____   17. _____
8. _____   18. _____
9. _____   19. _____
10. _____   20. _____

UNIT 5 Communication • **Lesson 3** *Breaking into Print: Before and After the Invention of the Printing Press*

▶ **Words with *-ly***

Strategies

Meaning Strategy Complete each sentence with a word from the parentheses.

21. A police investigation is conducted in _____ . (secret, secretly)

22. It started raining _____ . (suddenly, sudden)

23. Helping a blind person across an unfamiliar street is a

_____ action. (kind, kindly)

24. Most students would _____ take a vacation. (gladly, glad)

25. A mouse can move around _____ . (quiet, quietly)

26. We should display our awards _____ . (proud, proudly)

27. People who work hard are _____ to succeed. (like, likely)

28. A submarine can go _____ into the ocean. (deep, deeply)

29. A mountain climber is very _____ . (bold, boldly)

30. Cheetahs are animals that move very _____ . (quickly, quick)

SPELLING

Name _____ Date _____

UNIT 5 Communication • **Lesson 4** *Koko's Kitten*

Homographs

> **Homographs** are words that are spelled the same but have different meanings and origins.
>
> **Vocabulary Words**
> ▶ **present:** not absent
> ▶ **sole:** type of fish
> ▶ **poker:** a rod for stirring fire
> ▶ **object:** a thing
> ▶ **entrance:** delight; charm

Write another meaning for these words.

1. present   _____

2. sole   _____

3. poker   _____

4. object   _____

5. entrance   _____

Practice

The words in the sentences are underlined twice because they have different meanings. Write the meaning of each underlined word in the sentences. You should have two different meanings for each sentence.

Example: The doctor <u>wound</u> a bandage around her <u>wound</u>.
wound—wrapped around   *wound*—an injury

The person who placed <u>second</u> was only a <u>second</u> away from winning the race.

6. _____   7. _____

I jumped back as I <u>saw</u> the <u>saw</u> moving toward my hand.

8. _____   9. _____

The <u>swallow</u> fell off the tree as it tried to <u>swallow</u> its food.

10. _____   11. _____

Fishermen sit in a <u>row</u> as they <u>row</u> their fishing boat.

12. _____   13. _____

The man took a <u>rest</u> after doing the <u>rest</u> of his work.

14. _____   15. _____

The judge at the <u>fair</u> made a <u>fair</u> decision.

16. _____   17. _____

The <u>pupil</u> had a speck of dirt in the <u>pupil</u> of her eye.

18. _____   19. _____

There was a <u>rank</u> odor coming from the <u>rank</u> of garbage bags.

20. _____   21. _____

VOCABULARY

Words with *-ful* or *-less*

Word List

1. sightless
2. careless
3. painless
4. hopeless
5. homeless
6. useless
7. skillful
8. thankful
9. powerful
10. respectful
11. thoughtful
12. helpful
13. fearful
14. joyful
15. playful

Selection Words

16. restless
17. tailless
18. mouthful
19. distressful
20. healthful

Pattern Study

The suffix *-less* means "without;" the suffix *-ful* means "full of."

▶ Use the definitions that are given to you to write the meaning of each spelling word. The first one is done for you.

1. sight: to see

   sightless *without sight or not being able to see*

2. care: to pay close and serious attention

   careless _____

3. pain: a feeling of being hurt

   painless _____

4. hope: to wish for something very much

   hopeless _____

5. home: the place where a person lives

   homeless _____

6. use: having a particular purpose

   useless _____

7. rest: stopping of activity

   restless _____

UNIT 5 Communication • **Lesson 4** *Koko's Kitten*

▶ **Words with** *-ful* **or** *-less*

Strategies

Family Strategy Use your knowledge of suffixes to determine the meaning of each word. If you need help, use a dictionary.

8. thought: the act of thinking

thoughtful _____

9. help: to give or do something useful

helpful _____

10. fear: a feeling caused by knowing danger or pain is near

fearful _____

11. joy: a strong feeling of happiness or delight

joyful _____

12. play: activity that is done for fun

playful _____

13. skill: the power or ability to do something

skillful _____

14. thank: to say that one is grateful

thankful _____

15. mouth: the opening through which animals take food

mouthful _____

SPELLING

> A **simile** is a comparison between two things using the words *like* or *as*.
>
> The rumble of hooves sounded like distant thunder.
>
> **Vocabulary Words**
> ▶ **honey:** a thick sweet liquid made by bees
> ▶ **substance:** the material that something is made of
> ▶ **sparkled:** shone in quick bright flashes
> ▶ **diamond:** a mineral that is in the clear or crystal form
> ▶ **skinny:** very thin

 **Write an explanation for each simile. The first one is done for you.**

1. The professor is as <u>dull as dishwater</u>.

   The professor is very boring.

2. My hands are as <u>cold as ice</u>.

   _____

3. Her smile <u>sparkled like a pair of diamond earrings</u>.

   _____

4. Brice is as <u>skinny as a rail</u>.

   _____

5. Lina is as <u>strong as an ox</u>.

   _____

▶ Simile

Practice

Use the sentences to create similes. The first one is done for you.

6. Pancakes are usually flat.

Hana's stomach is as flat as a pancake.

7. A mouse can be very quiet.

_____

8. The ocean is very deep.

_____

9. A hyena's laugh can be scary.

_____

10. A snail moves very slowly.

_____

Complete each simile.

Example: "as quiet as a *mouse*"

11. "sleeps like a _____"

12. "swims like a _____"

13. "as rich as _____"

14. "as slow as _____"

15. "soars like a _____"

VOCABULARY

Words with ex-

Word List

1. except
2. example
3. extend
4. excellent
5. exchange
6. exclaim
7. exclude
8. excuse
9. explain
10. expensive
11. express
12. extreme
13. expand
14. exhaust
15. explore

Selection Words

16. exactly
17. expecting
18. experiments
19. excited
20. exhibit

Pattern Study

> ex- means "former," "outside," or "outer."

▶ Complete each sentence with a word from the box.

1. The store is open every day _____ Sunday.

2. Please _____ your left hand.

3. My friend and I _____ recipes for dessert.

4. You have the right to _____ your opinion.

5. We do not _____ anyone from our club.

6. Please _____ his bad manners.

7. The sailors set out to _____ the uncharted waters.

8. My best friend lives at the _____ end of the block.

9. Metal will _____ if it is heated.

10. We _____ ourselves when we do many things at the same time.

11. I saw an _____ of African art at the museum.

▶ **Words with ex-**

Strategies

 Meaning Strategy Use the story "Louis Braille: The Boy Who Invented Books for the Blind" to help you learn the meanings of the following words. Complete each sentence with one word from the parentheses.

12. Louis was one of the best students in his class; he was an

_____ student. (excellent, excited)

13. "Raised-print" is an _____ of a type of reading pattern for the blind. (example, examine)

14. The school library at Louis Braille's school had

_____ fourteen books for the blind. (exactly, exhibit)

15. "Raised-print books were very _____ to make." (exchange, expensive)

16. Louis tried to _____ to his friends that it was important to invent another way to teach people who are blind how to read. (explain, excuse)

17. Louis was _____ when he learned he was going to meet Captain Barbier, the man who invented the nightwriting technique. (excited, exhaust)

18. "Captain Barbier had been _____ to see a man, not a twelve-year-old boy!" (extend, expecting)

19. Louis tried to _____ ways to perfect Captain Barbier's nightwriting technique. (explore, examine)

20. Louis conducted many _____ on ways to improve Captain Barbier's writing technique. (experiments, explore)

SPELLING

UNIT 5 Communication • **Lesson 6** *My Two Drawings*

▶ Review

> **Homographs** are words that have the same spelling, different meanings, and different origins.
>
>   **object:** a thing   **object:** to protest
>
> **Use these words to complete the exercise below.**
>
> ▶ **sledge:** heavy hammer
> ▶ **lean:** not fat
> ▶ **meal:** ground grain
> ▶ **miss:** unmarried woman or girl
> ▶ **seal:** a mark of ownership
>
> A **descriptive word** is a word that is used to describe a person, place, thing, or idea.

Write another meaning for each word.

1. sledge _____

2. lean _____

3. meal _____

4. miss _____

5. seal _____

Complete each sentence with a descriptive word from the parentheses.

6. The fitness trainer had _____ muscles. (firm, creepy)

7. The _____ army was welcomed home. (lazy, victorious)

UNIT 5 Communication • **Lesson 6** *My Two Drawings*

Practice

| creepy | tiresome | marvelous | plenty | magnificent |

Complete each sentence with a descriptive word. Use a dictionary to learn the meaning of the descriptive word before completing the sentence.

8. This building has a _____ design.

9. My two-year-old brother is _____.

10. I had a _____ feeling after hearing the ghost story.

11. I went to a _____ birthday party.

12. There is _____ of milk left.

Read the given sentence, then write another sentence using the underlined homograph. The sentence should contain a different meaning from the underlined homograph.

13. Did you <u>ring</u> the doorbell?

   _____

14. White clothes <u>soil</u> easily.

   _____

15. We ate <u>squash</u> for dinner.

   _____

VOCABULARY

UNIT 5 Communication • **Lesson 6** *My Two Drawings*

Review: Words with *re-*, *-ture*, *-ful*, and *-ly*

Word List

1. reverse
2. review
3. report
4. repackage
5. powerful
6. nature
7. kindly
8. lately
9. loyally
10. gladly
11. skillful
12. barely
13. helpful
14. painful
15. furniture

Selection Words

16. texture
17. adventure
18. future
19. friendly
20. reward

Pattern Study

The prefix **re-** and the suffixes **-ful** and **-ly** can be added to words without changing the base word.

▶ Write the words with **re-**.

1. _____ 4. _____

2. _____ 5. _____

3. _____

▶ Write the words ending with **-ture**.

6. _____ 9. _____

7. _____ 10. _____

8. _____

▶ Write the words with the suffix **-ly**.

11. _____ 14. _____

12. _____ 15. _____

13. _____ 16. _____

▶ Write the words with suffix **-ful**.

17. _____ 19. _____

18. _____ 20. _____

UNIT 5   Communication • **Lesson 6** *My Two Drawings*

Words with *re-, -ture, -ful,* and *-ly*

Strategies

Conventions Strategy Add the suffixes *-ly* or *-ful*, or the prefix *re-* to each word part to create a spelling word. The first one is done for you.

	-ly	*-ful*	*re-*
21. help	_____	*helpful*	_____
22. ward	_____	_____	_____
23. late	_____	_____	_____
24. pain	_____	_____	_____
25. power	_____	_____	_____
26. skill	_____	_____	_____
27. loyal	_____	_____	_____
28. glad	_____	_____	_____
29. bare	_____	_____	_____
30. verse	_____	_____	_____

Family Strategy Use your knowledge of suffixes to write three words that are related to the word provided. The first one is done for you.

31. review *reviewer, reviewing, reviewed*

32. report _____

33. record _____

34. help _____

SPELLING

UNIT 6 A Changing America • **Lesson 1** *Early America*

Classification

> **Classification** is arranging things in groups.
> For example, *donkey, elephant,* and *zebra* can all be
> classified as animals.

 **Try It!** Use the story "Early America" to answer
these questions.

1. Write the names of two ancient civilizations that existed in
   North and South America.

   (page 484) _____

   _____

2. The first European countries to build settlements in the

   United States were: (page 485) _____

   _____

3. Name the states or places where early settlers created

   colonies. (page 486) _____

   _____

4. Name some of the Native American tribes that existed.

   (page 487) _____

   _____

5. Why did early settlers move to the Americas?

   (pages 484, 485) _____

   _____

UNIT 6 A Changing America • **Lesson 1** *Early America*

▶**Classification**

Practice

Ireland	Germany	Taiwan	Japan
Togo	Malaysia	Sudan	Canada
France	Mexico	India	Mozambique
Ghana	Spain	Vietnam	United States
Croatia	Sierra Leone	Pakistan	Zimbabwe

Use an atlas to complete this exercise. Your teacher has already shown you the location of the continents and some of the different countries located on these continents.

Write the countries that are located in Europe.

6. _____   9. _____

7. _____   10. _____

8. _____

Write the countries that are located in Asia.

11. _____   14. _____

12. _____   15. _____

13. _____   16. _____

Write the countries that are located in Africa.

17. _____   20. _____

18. _____   21. _____

19. _____   22. _____

Write the countries that are located in North America.

23. _____   25. _____

24. _____

VOCABULARY

UNIT 6 A Changing America • **Lesson 1** *Early America*

Rhyming Words

Word List

1. blob
2. club
3. fail
4. sum
5. hail
6. stub
7. gum
8. mail
9. drum
10. hum
11. snob
12. pail
13. glum
14. snip
15. trip

Selection Words

16. grub
17. chip
18. drip
19. bail
20. plum

Pattern Study

> A vowel between two consonants usually has a short-vowel sound.

▶ Write the **CVC** or **CCVC** pattern for each word that rhymes with *slob*.

1. _____   2. _____

▶ Write the **CVC** or **CCVC** pattern for each word that rhymes with *cub*.

3. _____   5. _____

4. _____

▶ Write the **CVC** or **CCVC** pattern for each word that rhymes with *mum*.

6. _____   9. _____

7. _____   10. _____

8. _____   11. _____

▶ Write the **CVC** or **CCVC** pattern for each word that rhymes with *ship*.

12. _____   14. _____

13. _____   15. _____

▶ Write four words that rhyme with *rail*.

16. _____   18. _____

17. _____   19. _____

UNIT 6 A Changing America • **Lesson 1** *Early America*

▶Rhyming Words

Strategies

 Rhyming Strategy   **Complete the group of letters with the *ank* ending to create a word.**

20. pl _____

21. s _____

22. r _____

23. th _____

24. dr _____

Complete the group of letters with the *ock* ending to create a word.

25. l _____

26. st _____

27. s _____

28. d _____

29. r _____

Complete the group of letters with the *ash* ending to create a word.

30. cr _____

31. spl _____

32. d _____

33. r _____

34. b _____

SPELLING

UNIT 6 A Changing America • **Lesson 2** *The Voyage of the Mayflower*

Analogies

An **analogy** is two pairs of words that are related in the same way.

Front is to **back** as **left** is to **right**.

Front is the opposite of **back** and **left** is the opposite of **right**.

Use the vocabulary words to practice analogies.

▶ **vessel:** a ship or large boat

▶ **provision:** something fit to be eaten

▶ **carpenter:** a person who builds and repairs houses and other things made of wood

▶ **masts:** tall pole on a sailing ship or boat that supports the sails and rigging

▶ **timber:** wood that is used in building things; lumber

 **Try It!** Complete each analogy with a word from the parentheses.

1. **Vessel** is to **ship** as **aircraft** is to _____.
   (wings, airplane, plants)

2. **Provision** is to **food** as **steal** is to _____.
   (take, thief, not yours)

3. **Carpenter** is to **wood** as **plumber** is to _____.
   (dry, pipes, wrench)

4. **Masts** are to **ship** as **tires** are to _____.
   (walks, roles, cars)

5. **Timber** is to **wood** as **iron** is to _____.
   (metal, wood, rail)

Name _____ Date _____

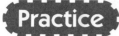

Complete each analogy with a word from the box.

chirp	speak	see

Object-Action

6. **Dog** is to **bark** as **bird** is to _____.

7. **Ear** is to **hear** as **mouth** is to _____.

8. **Nose** is to **smell** as **eye** is to _____.

sea	hive	pen

Place

9. **Bear** is to **den** as **bee** is to _____.

10. **Bird** is to **sky** as **fish** is to _____.

11. **Dog** is to **kennel** as **pig** is to _____.

vegetable	money	fish	shape

Object class

12. **Rose** is to **flower** as **dollar** is to _____.

13. **Blue** is to **color** as **round** is to _____.

14. **Dog** is to **animal** as **carrot** is to _____.

15. **Parrot** is to **bird** as **shark** is to _____.

VOCABULARY

UNIT 6 A Changing America • **Lesson 2** *The Voyage of the Mayflower*

Words with -ing

Pattern Study

Word List

1. biking
2. boating
3. bowling
4. building
5. camping
6. climbing
7. dancing
8. exploring
9. fishing
10. golfing
11. jogging
12. napping
13. painting
14. practicing
15. reading

Selection Words

16. capsizing
17. howling
18. sinking
19. crossing
20. planking

When a base word ends with *e*, you drop the *e* before adding **-ing.**

If a word has one syllable and ends with a short vowel and consonant, double the final consonant before adding **-ing.**

The **-ing** ending shows something is happening now.

Write the base word for each spelling word.

1. _____bike_____   11. _____
2. _____   12. _____
3. _____   13. _____
4. _____   14. _____
5. _____   15. _____
6. _____   16. _____
7. _____   17. _____
8. _____   18. _____
9. _____   19. _____
10. _____   20. _____

UNIT 6 A Changing America • **Lesson 2** *The Voyage of the Mayflower*

Words with *-ing*

Strategies

Conventions Strategy Circle the misspelled word in the sentence and write the correct spelling on the lines provided. If the sentence is correct, leave the line blank.

21. Exploreing ancient caves can be scary. _____

22. Boatting on the bay is fun. _____

23. A bikeing marathon can last for a long time.

_____

24. You can see people joging on warm evenings.

_____

25. I am paintting my room. _____

26. There is a man walkeing on the other side of the street.

_____

27. Some people take classes on ballroom danceing.

_____

28. A campping trip can be an adventure. _____

29. I will do my homework after I wake up from naping.

_____

30. Playing the piano is a skill that requires practicing.

_____

SPELLING

UNIT 6 A Changing America • **Lesson 3** *Pocahontas*

Levels of Specificity

> **Levels of Specificity** are words that fall within categories.
>
> Writers use it to describe things in more specific terms. For example, you could say, "My pet <u>dog</u> has curly fur on its tail." Or, you could say, "My pet <u>poodle</u> has curly fur on its tail." The second word is more specific and is therefore a better description.

Read the sentences and complete the exercise below.

Earth is a planet.
Every country is located in a continent.
Los Angeles is a city in California.
Miami is a city in Florida.

Write the words in order of specificity.

planet	continent	Earth
1. _____	_____	_____
country	city	state
2. _____	_____	_____
country	continent	state
3. _____	_____	_____
United States	California	Los Angeles
4. _____	_____	_____
Miami	United States	Florida
5. _____	_____	_____

UNIT 6 A Changing America • **Lesson 3** *Pocahontas*

▶ **Levels of Specificity**

VOCABULARY

Practice

pills	pearls
rocking chair	biology
station wagon	penguin
fruit	cat
math class	great white shark

Complete each group of words with a more specific word from the box to show how the words relate. Explain your answers to other students.

6. living things, mammal, _____

7. jewelry, necklace, _____

8. furniture, chair, _____

9. vehicle, car, _____

10. subject, science, _____

11. medicine, _____, aspirin

12. _____, melon, watermelon

13. fish, shark, _____

14. animal, bird, _____

15. education, school, _____

UNIT 6 A Changing America • **Lesson 3** *Pocahontas*

Words with -er or -est

Word List

1. chillier
2. dirtier
3. dizzier
4. drowsiest
5. emptier
6. gloomier
7. heaviest
8. hungrier
9. noisier
10. windiest
11. prettiest
12. ugliest
13. healthier
14. foggier
15. friskiest

Selection Words

16. cloudier
17. crispier
18. fanciest
19. juicier
20. creamier

Pattern Study

The suffix *-er* means "more" and the suffix *-est* means "most."

If a word ends in *e*, drop the *e* before adding *-er* or *-est*. If a word ends with a short vowel and a consonant, double the consonant before adding *-er* or *-est*. If a word ends in *y*, change the *y* to *i* before adding *-er* or *-est*.

Remove the suffix *-er* or *-est* from each spelling word to create a base word.

1. _____ 11. _____

2. _____ 12. _____

3. _____ 13. _____

4. _____ 14. _____

5. _____ 15. _____

6. _____ 16. _____

7. _____ 17. _____

8. _____ 18. _____

9. _____ 19. _____

10. _____ 20. _____

UNIT 6 A Changing America • **Lesson 3** *Pocahontas*

▶ Words with -er or -est

Strategies

Meaning Strategy **Complete each sentence with a word from the parentheses.**

21. He felt too _____ to walk after the ride.
(dizzy, dizzier, dizziest)

22. People who are very _____ shouldn't drive cars. (drowsy, drowsier, drowsiest)

23. The _____ days of all come during winter. (gloomy, gloomier, gloomiest)

24. Children are usually _____ than adults. (noisy, noisier, noisiest)

25. Chicago is a very _____ city. (windy, windier, windiest)

26. That is the _____ dress I've ever seen. (pretty, prettier, prettiest)

27. I have an _____ scar on my hand. (ugly, uglier, ugliest)

28. That's the _____ puppy I have ever seen. (frisky, friskier, friskiest)

29. Today was _____ than yesterday. (cloudy, cloudier, cloudiest)

30. Movie stars wear _____ clothes. (fancy, fancier, fanciest)

SPELLING

Latin Roots

Many of the English words we use every day contain parts, or roots, that have been borrowed from much older languages. For example, English words often have roots from the ancient languages of Greek and Latin. These roots may be found in a variety of words, and have the same meaning no matter where you find them. When you know the meaning of a Latin root, you can begin to figure out the meaning of the English word that contains it. Here are some common Latin roots and their meanings:

trans = "across"   *cred* = "believe"   *aud* = "hear"

hosp = "host"   *anim* = "life"   *cap* = "head"

dent = "tooth"   *doc* = "teach"

The word *dentist* has the Latin root *dent,* which means "tooth." You can tell from the meaning of the Latin root that a dentist is a person who takes care of your teeth. The word *captain* contains the Latin root *cap,* which means "head." You can tell from the meaning of the Latin root that a captain is someone who is the head, or leader, of something, such as a ship.

 **Try It!** **Read the following Latin roots and their meanings. Write another word containing each Latin root beside the one provided.**

1. *act:* "do"; actor _____

2. *struct:* "build"; structure _____

3. *mot:* "move"; motion _____

4. *mem:* "mindful of"; memory _____

5. *volv:* "roll"; evolve _____

UNIT 6 A Changing America • **Lesson 4** *Martha Helps the Rebel*

▶ **Latin Roots**

Practice

The following groups of words all have the same Latin roots. Circle the root that each word has in common. Then examine each word carefully and think of its meaning. Think about what the meanings have in common. Then choose a definition for the root from the box below and write it in the blank.

sea	alone	to see	empty	move

6. vision, visible, invisible, visual

The Latin root is *vis*. What does *vis* mean? _____

7. solo, solitary, solitude

The Latin root is *sol*. What does *sol* mean? _____

8. marine, marina, submarine

The Latin root is *mar*. What does *mar* mean? _____

9. mobility, mobile, automobile

The Latin root is *mob*. What does *mob* mean? _____

10. vacant, vacancy, vacuum

The Latin root is *vac*. What does *vac* mean? _____

UNIT 6 A Changing America • **Lesson 4** *Martha Helps the Rebel*

Latin Roots

Word List

1. fact
2. factor
3. manufacture
4. factory
5. satisfaction
6. obtain
7. entertain
8. maintain
9. contain
10. motel
11. motor
12. promote
13. remote
14. motion
15. porter

Selection Words

16. transport
17. portable
18. import
19. important
20. support

Pattern Study

Many English words contain **Latin roots,** or word parts that have meaning. If you know the spellings and meanings of common Latin roots, you can spell and define words that contain Latin roots. The spelling words have these Latin roots:

fac, meaning "make" or "do"

tain, meaning "hold"

mot, meaning "move"

port, meaning "carry"

1. Write the spelling words with the Latin root *mot*.

_____ _____ _____

_____ _____

2. Write the spelling words with the Latin root *tain*.

_____ _____ _____

_____

3. Write the spelling words with the Latin root *port*.

_____ _____ _____

_____ _____

4. Write the spelling words with the Latin root *fac*.

_____ _____

_____

▶ Latin Roots

SPELLING

Strategies

Pronunciation Strategy Write each spelling word next to its pronunciation from the dictionary.

5. mo′ tər _____

6. ri port′ _____

7. fak′ tə rē _____

8. kən tān′ _____

9. mō′ shən _____

10. mō tel′ _____

11. en tər tān′ _____

12. trans pôrt′ _____

13. sə pôrt′ _____

14. əb tān′ _____

15. fakt _____

Meaning Strategy Write the spelling word next to its definition.

16. Able to be carried from place to place _____

17. Far away _____

18. A feeling of comfort and pleasure _____

19. To make something _____

20. A person who carries baggage _____

Name _____ Date _____

Greek Roots

English words also contain parts, or roots, that have been borrowed from the ancient language of Greek. When you know the meaning of a **Greek root,** you can begin to figure out the meaning of the English word that contains it. Here are some common Greek roots and their meanings:

micro = small	*tele* = far off	*graph* = to write
bio = life	*geo* = earth	*astr* = star
log = word	*phon* = sounds	

The word *telephone* has the Greek roots *tele* and *phon,* which mean "far off" and "sounds." You can tell from the meaning of the Greek roots that a telephone is a device that allows you to hear sounds from far off.

Read the following Greek roots and their meanings. Write another word containing each Greek root beside the one provided.

1. *meter:* "measure"; centimeter _____

2. *cycl:* "circle"; tricycle _____

3. *astr:* "star"; astronomy _____

4. *micro:* "small"; microscope _____

5. *graph:* "to write"; telegraph _____

▶ **Greek Roots**

Practice

The following groups of words all have the same Greek roots. Circle the root that each word has in common. Then examine each word carefully and think of its meaning. Think about what the meanings have in common. Then choose a definition for the root from the box below and write it in the blank.

heat	word	see	to write

6. diagram: a plan or sketch
telegram: a message
grammar: rules about writing

The Greek root is **gram.** What does **gram** mean? _____

7. telescope: allows you to see distant things
microscope: allows you to see tiny things
periscope: allows you to see above the water
while in a submarine

The Greek root is **scop.** What does **scop** mean? _____

8. thermos: keeps liquids hot
thermometer: measures how hot or cold something is
thermostat: controls the heater

The Greek root is **therm.** What does **therm** mean? _____

9. dialogue: words exchanged between people
monologue: a speech given by a single person in a play
apology: words spoken to say you are sorry

The Greek root is **log.** What does **log** mean? _____

VOCABULARY

Greek Roots

Word List

1. autograph
2. graphics
3. geography
4. paragraph
5. photograph
6. phonograph
7. graph
8. apology
9. technology
10. geology
11. biology
12. bicycle
13. tricycle
14. recycle
15. motorcycle

Selection Words

16. telegraph
17. television
18. telethon
19. telegram
20. telescope

Pattern Study

Many English words contain **Greek roots.** If you know the spellings and meanings of common Greek roots, you can figure out how to spell and define words with these roots.

The Greek root *graph* means "to write."

The Greek root *logy* means "to speak."

The Greek root *cycl* means "circle."

The Greek root *tele* means "far off."

1. Write the spelling words with the Greek root *tele.*

_____   _____   _____

_____   _____

2. Write the spelling words with the Greek root *logy.*

_____   _____   _____

_____

3. Write the spelling words with the Greek root *cycl.*

_____   _____   _____

_____

4. Write the spelling words with the Greek root *graph.*

_____   _____   _____

_____   _____   _____

_____

UNIT 6 A Changing America • **Lesson 5** *Going West*

▶ **Greek Roots**

{ **Strategies** }

Meaning Strategy Write the spelling word next to its definition.

5. A person's signature _____

6. A vehicle with three wheels _____

7. The science dealing with the surface of Earth _____

8. A group of sentences about the same topic _____

9. A picture that is made by a camera _____

10. Saying you are sorry _____

11. The study of living things _____

12. The study of rocks and minerals _____

13. To use something over again _____

14. A device used to look at the stars _____

15. A message sent by a telegraph _____

SPELLING

Classification and Levels of Specificity

Classification means putting related things into groups, or categories. Cars, trucks, and airplanes can be classified as vehicles. Poodles, German shepherds, and Irish setters can be classified as dogs.

An idea related to classification is **Levels of Specificity**. In the classifications above, *vehicle* and *dog* are the general categories, while *cars* and *poodles* are more specific items within each category. Ideas can become more specific as you use more specific words to describe them. Each word in the following groups is more specific than the previous one:

object, vehicle, truck

animal, dog, German shepherd

When you are writing, try to use more specific words. The sentence "I walked the German shepherd" is much more interesting than "I walked the dog."

The following groups of specific words all belong in the same category. Write the category on the lines that follow.

1. flute, drums, trumpet _____

2. bananas, peaches, pears _____

3. aqua, lavender, gray _____

4. pen, pencil, marker _____

UNIT 6 A Changing America • **Lesson 6** *The California Gold Rush*

Classification and Levels of Specificity

Practice

The following groups of specific words all belong in the same category. Write the category on the lines that follow.

5. beef, pork, chicken _____

6. spider, centipede, beetle _____

7. lake, river, creek _____

8. Spain, Italy, Greece _____

9. books, magazines, newspapers _____

10. east, southwest, north, _____

| spaghetti | dessert | daisy | German shepherd | bongo |
| grizzly | jigsaw | cockatoo | orangutan | seasoning |

Complete each group with a word from the box.

11. plant   flower   _____

12. game   puzzle   _____ puzzle

13. _____   cake   sponge cake

14. _____   pepper   cayenne pepper

15. food   Italian food   _____

16. musical instrument   drum   _____ drum

17. bird   parrot   _____

18. animal   dog   _____

19. animal   bear   _____ bear

20. animal   monkey   _____

VOCABULARY

UNIT 6 A Changing America • **Lesson 6** *The California Gold Rush*

Review: -er, -est, and -ing

Word List

1. climbing
2. dancing
3. exploring
4. fishing
5. golfing
6. chillier
7. dirtiest
8. dizziest
9. drowsier
10. emptying
11. gloomier
12. heaviest
13. prettier
14. noisier
15. windiest

Selection Words

16. liveliest
17. curlier
18. speediest
19. sweatiest
20. filthier

Pattern Study

The endings **-er** and **-est** are added to words to show comparisons, as in *whiter* and *whitest*. Drop the silent *e* at the end of a word before adding **-er** or **-est**.

The ending **-ing** is added to a word to show an action that is happening in the present. Drop the silent *e* at the end of a word before adding **-ing**.

▶ Write the base word for the spelling words that end in *-ing*.

1. _____   4. _____

2. _____   5. _____

3. _____   6. _____

▶ Add the suffixes **-er** or **-est** to the following words to write the spelling words.

7. chilly _____   14. noisy _____

8. dirty _____   15. windy _____

9. dizzy _____   16. lively _____

10. drowsy _____   17. curly _____

11. gloomy _____   18. speedy _____

12. heavy _____   19. sweaty _____

13. pretty _____   20. filthy _____

UNIT 6 A Changing America • **Lesson 6** *The California Gold Rush*

Words with -er, -est, and -ing

Strategies

Meaning Strategy Complete each sentence with a word from the parentheses.

21. I want to _____ the caves by the ocean.
(exploring, explore)

22. My dad and I go _____ on Sundays.
(golf, golfing)

23. The clothes in the hamper are the _____.
(dirty, dirtiest)

24. Is your brother doing his chores and _____
the trash cans? (empty, emptying)

25. Rainy days are _____ than sunny days.
(gloomier, gloomiest)

26. A pony is _____ than a lizard.
(pretty, prettier)

27. We need a _____ day for flying kites.
(windy, windiest)

28. The band played _____ tunes all night long.
(lively, liveliest)

29. Mary has _____ locks of hair that flow down
her back. (curly, curlier)

30. Ramon made a _____ recovery after he broke
his leg. (speedy, speediest)

SPELLING

Name _____ Date _____

Review

You will remember that Greek and Latin roots are units of meaning that can be found in the English language. As the English language was being formed, word parts were borrowed from the ancient languages of Latin and Greek.

Some Greek and Latin roots are prefixes and come at the beginnings of words. There is a special set of these prefixes that mean numbers:

uni = one	***bi*** = two	***tri*** = three
quad = four	***pent*** = five	***hex*** = six
hept = seven	***oct*** = eight	***non*** = nine
dec = ten		

The word *decade* contains the prefix ***dec,*** which means "ten." A decade is a period of time equaling ten years. If you know the meaning of a number prefix, you can begin to figure out the meaning of a word with that prefix.

 **Fill in each blank with the meaning of the number prefix.**

1. An **octagon** is a shape with _____ sides.

2. A **tricycle** is a bike with _____ wheels.

3. A **unicorn** is a horse in legends with _____ horn.

4. A **quadruped** is an animal with _____ feet.

5. A **decathlon** is a sports contest with _____ events.

UNIT 6 A Changing America • **Lesson 7** *The Golden Spike*

▶**Review**

Practice

Now that you know the meanings of the words with number prefixes on the previous page, use each word in a sentence of your own.

6. octagon: _____

_____

_____

7. tricycle: _____

_____

_____

8. unicorn: _____

_____

_____

9. quadruped: _____

_____

_____

10. decathlon: _____

_____

_____

VOCABULARY

UNIT 6 A Changing America • **Lesson 7** *The Golden Spike*

Review: Greek and Latin Roots

High Frequency

1. autograph
2. graphics
3. geography
4. paragraph
5. photograph
6. phonograph
7. transport
8. portable
9. import
10. important
11. support
12. remote
13. motor
14. motel
15. porter

Selection Words

16. biology
17. apology
18. technology
19. geology
20. graph

Pattern Study

Learning the meaning of a root will help you decode the meaning of an unfamiliar word that contains that root.

1. Write the words that contain the root **graph**, meaning "to write."

   _____ _____ _____

   _____ _____ _____

   _____

2. Write the words that contain the root **port**, meaning "to carry."

   _____ _____ _____

   _____ _____ _____

3. Write the words that contain the root **mot**, meaning "to move."

   _____ _____ _____

4. Write the words that contain the root **logy**, meaning "to speak."

   _____ _____ _____

   _____

UNIT 6 A Changing America • **Lesson 7** *The Golden Spike*

▶**Greek and Latin Roots**

Strategies

 Dictionary Strategy Use a dictionary to find the meanings of the spelling words in the box. Then complete each sentence with the correct spelling word.

geology	remote	autograph
motel	biology	graphics
phonograph	technology	porter
geography	paragraph	

5. A person's signature is an _____.

6. _____ have to do with pictures and designs.

7. A _____ is a record player.

8. The study of living things is _____.

9. Methods and devices that are used in science are part of

_____.

10. We study about rocks, mountains, and cliffs in _____.

11. The study of people and countries is _____.

12. Something that is far away is _____.

13. We stayed at a _____ while on vacation.

14. A _____ is a person who carries baggage.

15. Begin a _____ with a topic sentence.

SPELLING

Vocabulary Rules

Synonyms are words that are similar in meaning.

> The solution to the puzzle is **easy.**
> The solution to the puzzle is **simple.**

Antonyms are words that are opposite in meaning.

> An elephant is a **large** animal.
> A mouse is a **small** animal.

Homophones are words that are pronounced alike but are spelled differently and have different meanings.

> The wind **blew** white clouds across the **blue** sky.

Some common homophones are **their/there/they're; your/you're;** and **it's/its.**

- *Their* means "belonging to them." *There* means "in that place," or it may be used at the beginning of a sentence with *is, are, was,* or *were. They're* is a contraction for "they are."

  > **They're** happy that **their** team won over **there.**

- *Your* is a possessive pronoun meaning "belonging to you." *You're* is a contraction for "you are."

  > **You're** sure **your** team won?

- *Its* is a possessive pronoun meaning "belonging to it." *It's* is a contraction for "it is."

  > **It's** a shame that the tree lost **its** leaves so soon.

Context Clues

When you come to a new word in your reading, you can sometimes figure out the meaning of the word from its context, or the words and sentences around it. Writers give context clues in five main ways.

▶ **Definition** The meaning of the word is stated.

> Mother ordered a *cushion*, which is a **soft pillow.**

▶ **Example** The meaning of the unfamiliar word is explained through examples.

> Her *interjections*—**Ouch! Wow!**—are so dramatic.

▶ **Comparison** The unfamiliar word is similar to a familiar word or phrase.

> Why would I *retract* my statement? I will not **withdraw** it.

▶ **Contrast** The unfamiliar word is opposite a familiar word or phrase.

> She is really a *novice*, although she appears **experienced.**

▶ **Cause and Effect** The unfamiliar word is explained as part of a cause-and-effect relationship.

> He really enjoyed the *hors d'oeuvres* tonight because he always has a **snack** before dinner.

Multiple-Meaning Words

Multiple-meaning words are words that have the same spelling and pronunciation but have more than one meaning and may be different parts of speech in different situations.

> **gorge**
> Noun: **a deep, narrow valley with steep sides**
> Verb: **to eat greedily**

Word Roots

A word root is the main part of a word. Sometimes a prefix or suffix is added to it. These additions often change a word's meaning or its part of speech.

> **Audio** means "hear."

> An **audio**tape is a tape you **listen** to.
> An **audi**ence is a group that **hears** a performance.
> **Audio**visual materials help us see and **hear** what we are learning.

Prefixes and Suffixes

- **Prefixes** are word parts added to the beginning of a root to change its meaning.

  > A **co**worker is a person with whom one works.
  > To **co**write is to write together.

- **Suffixes** are word parts added to the end of a root to change its meaning.

  > Fear**ful** means "full of fear."
  > A spoon**ful** is the amount that fills a spoon.

Spelling Strategies

There are many different ways to learn how to spell. A spelling strategy is a plan that can make learning to spell easier. Take some time to learn how these strategies can help you spell better.

Sound Pattern Strategies

Pronunciation Strategy

Learn to listen to the sounds in a word. Then spell each sound. *(sit)*

Consonant-Substitution Strategy

Try switching consonant letters without changing the vowel. *(bat, hat, rat, flat, splat)*

Vowel-Substitution Strategy

Try switching the vowel letters without changing the rest of the word. *(hit, hat, hut, hot)* / *(mane, mine)* / *(boat, beat)*

Rhyming Strategy

Think of a word that rhymes with the spelling word and has the same spelling pattern. *(cub, tub, rub)*

Structural Pattern Strategies

Conventions Strategy

Think about the rules and exceptions you have learned for adding endings to words. *(crying, cried)*

Visualization Strategy

Think about how the word looks. Most words look wrong when they do not have the right spelling. *(can*, not *cen)*

Proofreading Strategy

Check your writing carefully for spelling mistakes.

Meaning Pattern Strategies

Family Strategy

Think of how words from the same family are spelled. *(art, artist)*

Meaning Strategy

Think about the meaning of the word to make sure you're using the right word. *(see, sea)*

Compound Word Strategy

Break the compound into its two words to spell each word. *(homework, home work)*

Dictionary Strategy

Find the word in a dictionary to make sure your spelling is correct.

Spelling Rules

Short-Vowel Sound Spellings

Short-vowel sound spellings are more predictable than long-vowel sound spellings.

- Short-vowel sounds most often are found in words beginning with a vowel, such as *up*, *at*, and *end*, or words with *vowel-consonant* endings, such as *cup*, *bat*, and *lend*.
- Some short-vowel sounds are spelled with two or more letters, such as *bread* and *laugh*.
- Short vowels have many simple spelling patterns, such as *at*, *in*, *ot*, *et*, and *ug*.

The /a/ Sound

- /a/ is spelled *a*, as in *cat*.
- /a/ can also be spelled *a_e*, as in *have*.

The /e/ Sound

- /e/ is most often spelled *e*, as in *bed*.
- /e/ can be spelled *_ea_* in the middle of a word, as in *bread* or *head*.

The /i/ Sound

- /i/ is most often spelled *i*, as in *did*.
- When *y* is found in the middle of a word, it acts like a vowel. It usually makes the /i/ sound, as in *system*.
- /i/ is sometimes spelled *i_e*, as in the words *give* and *live*.

The /o/ Sound

- /o/ is usually spelled *o*, as in *got*.

The /u/ Sound

- /u/ is usually spelled *u*, as in *fun*.
- /u/ can be spelled *o*, as in *son*, or *o_e*, as in *glove*, *love*, and *come*.

Long-Vowel Sound Spellings

Long vowels sound like the letter names.
When long-vowel sounds are spelled with two vowels, the first vowel is usually heard and the second vowel is silent.

Vowel-consonant-e
- Many long-vowel sounds have the common *vowel-consonant-e* spelling pattern in which the *e* is silent, as in the word *date*.

The /ā/ Sound
- /ā/ is spelled *a, a_e, ai_,* and *_ay,* as in *agent, base, raid,* and *today.* The *ay* spelling is found at the end of words or syllables.

The /ē/ Sound
- /ē/ is often spelled *e, e_e, ee, ea,* and *_y* as in *be, here, agree, easy,* and *happy.*
- /ē/ is spelled *ei* in a few words such as *receive,* but also *_ie_* as in *pierce.* Remember the rhyme: "Write *i* before *e,* except after *c,* or when it sounds like /ā/ as in *neighbor* and *weigh.*"

The /ī/ Sound
- /ī/ is spelled *i, i_e, igh,* and *_y,* as in *icy, site, high,* and *dry.*

The /ō/ Sound
- /ō/ is spelled *o, o_e, oa_,* and *_ow,* as in *pony, bone, boat,* and *snow.*

The /ū/ Sound
- /ū/ is spelled *u, _ue,* or *u_e,* as in *unit, tissue,* and *cube.*

The /o͞o/ Sound
- /o͞o/ can be spelled *oo* in the middle of a word such as *tool, u* in the *u_e* pattern as in *tune,* or *_ew* at the end of a word such as *new.*

THE SCHWA SOUND

Unaccented syllables have a vowel sound called a schwa that is represented by a vowel. A variety of vowels can stand for the schwa sound. Visualizing how a word should look or over-pronouncing the ending as you spell it may help.

Schwa *-ant, -ent, -ance, -ence*
- The endings *-ant* and *-ent* add the meaning "one who" to a word.
- The endings *-ance* and *-ence* add the meaning "state or quality of" to a word.
- More words end in *-ent* and *-ence* than in *-ant* and *-ance*.
- Visualizing how the word should look can help you learn to spell words with these endings.

The /sh/ sound spelled *ti, ci, si*
- Drop the silent *e* before adding the ending.   *race, racial*
- Words that end in *c* or *ce* have the *ci* pattern.   *finance, financial*
- Words that end in *s* usually contain the *si* pattern.   *impress, impression*
- Words that end in *t* often have the *ti* pattern.   *reject, rejection*
- Some words have consonant spelling changes before the endings are added, such as *emit* and *emission*.

Schwa *-el, -al, -le, -il*
- Most of the time, the /əl/ sound at the end of a word is spelled *-le*.   *little, circle,*
- Verbs and action words that end with the /əl/ sound have the *-le* spelling.   *dazzle*
- Words that have the *-al* spelling for the /əl/ sound are usually nouns or adjectives (words that describe nouns).   *animal, petal final, signal*
- Words with final syllables that have the /əl/ sound can also be spelled *-el* or *-il*. Usually, these words are nouns.   *towel, label gerbil, pencil*
- In a few words, the /əl/ final syllable is spelled *-ol*.   *capitol*

STRUCTURAL SPELLING PATTERNS

Plurals
- Add -*s* to most nouns to make them plural. *(cat + s = cats)*
- Add -*es* to words that end in *ch, sh, s, ss, x, z,* or *zz.*
- Noticing the syllables in the singular and plural forms of a word can help you know whether to add -*s* or -*es*. When -*es* is added, it usually adds another syllable.

Irregular Plurals
- For words that end in *f* or *fe,* change the *f* to a *v* and add -*es.*
- Some plurals are spelled the same as the singular form, such as *deer.*
- The spelling changes in the plural form of some words, such as *tooth* and *teeth.*
- For a word that ends in *consonant-o,* add -*es.* If a word ends in *vowel-o,* -*s* is usually added.

Adding Endings
- For most words, endings are simply added to base words.
- If a word ends in *e* and the ending begins with a vowel, the *e* is dropped.
- When a word ends in *vowel-y,* just add the ending.

Adding -*ed* and -*ing*
- The ending -*ed* is added to most words to show an action that happened in the past.
- The ending -*ing* is added to a word to show an action that is happening in the present.
- Drop the silent *e* before adding -*ed* and -*ing* to words.

Adding -*er* and -*est*
- The endings -*er* and -*est* are added to words to show comparisons, such as *whiter* and *whitest.*
- Drop the silent *e* before adding these endings to words.

Changing *y* to *i*
- Notice the letter before the *y* in a word.
- When a word ends in *vowel-y,* just add the ending.
- When a word ends in *consonant-y,* change the *y* to *i* and add the ending.
- Do not change the *y* if the ending is -*ing.*

MEANING PATTERNS

Word Families *-ous*
- Words that end in *-ous* are common.
- If a word ends in *e,* drop the *e* before adding *-ous.*
- Change *y* to *i* before adding *-ous* to a word that ends in *y.*
- *-ous* added to a word creates an adjective.
- There are a few words with the soft *g* sound, as in *courageous,* in which the final *e* is not dropped.

Vowel-Sound Changes
- When the vowel sound in a base word changes because of an added ending, think of the base-word spelling and use the same vowel that is in the base word. *(major, majority)*

Contractions
- A contraction is a word formed from two or more words. When the words are joined together, some letters are taken out, and an apostrophe (') marks the place.
- Only one letter is taken out of some contractions.

I am – a = I'm

- Many letters are taken out of some contractions.

I would – woul = I'd

- The first word in the pair that makes a contraction usually keeps all of its letters.
- Entire words are left out of some contractions. *(of the clock – f* and *the = o'clock)*
- Some contractions are homophones. *(I'll, aisle; he'd, heed)*
- Make sure you put the apostrophe (') in the right place.
- Leaving out the apostrophe can result in a different word. The word *I'll* becomes the word *ill.*
- Only one contraction, *I'm,* is made with the word *am.*
- Only one contraction, *let's,* is made with the word *us.*
- Some contractions look the same, but mean two different things. *He'd* means "he would" and "he had."
- One contraction, *will not,* changes the spelling and the sound of the omitted letters to become *won't.*

Latin Spelling Patterns

- Latin roots are meaningful word parts that combine with words.

Root	Meaning
scribe, script	to write
form	a shape
sent, sens	to feel
rupt	to break
equa, equi	even
min	to make smaller
mit	to send
bene, beni	well
aud	to hear
port	to carry
dic, dict	to speak
gram	to write

- Some Latin patterns sound like others, which can make them tricky to spell.

Greek Spelling Patterns

- Understanding Greek word patterns and their meanings can help you spell many new words.

Root	Meaning
geo	earth
tele	far off
phon, phone	sounds
hydro	water
micro	small
aster, astr	star
centr	center
phobia	fear
graph	to write
bi, bio	life
cycl	circle
phys	nature
photo	light

- Many Greek roots spell the /f/ sound with the letters *ph*. When you hear the /f/ sound in an unfamiliar word with a Greek root, spell it with a *ph*.